Bittersweet

By Grace Augustine

No portions of this work may be reproduced without the express permission of the author.

Characters in this book are fiction and the figments of the author's imagination.

Edited by Shane Dayton

Cover Art by Brenton Ceaglske

Copyright@2013 by Grace Augustine

All rights reserved.

ISBN-13:978-1480198210

DEDICATION

For Deblyn…saying thank you for the inspiration to write and for your unending faithful friendship and love is not enough. Even in the midst of chaos and trying times, you still handle it all with such unending strength and panache!

CONTENTS

Acknowledgments

Chapter One

Chapter Two

Chapter Three

Chapter Four

Chapter Five

Chapter Six

Chapter Seven

Chapter Eight

Chapter Nine

Chapter Ten

Chapter Eleven

Chapter Twelve

Chapter Thirteen

Chapter Fourteen

Chapter Fifteen

Chapter Sixteen

Chapter Seventeen

Chapter Eighteen

Chapter Nineteen

Chapter Twenty

ACKNOWLEDGEMENTS

To Leslie, Amy, Jill, Mishelle and Drs. Guidici and Yacoub...thank you for teaching me how to handle my physical limitations and for showing me that holistic healthcare is what I need to manage my day to day adventures.

To my incredible team who made Bittersweet a reality...my amazing editor, Shane Dayton; photographer, Anna Beeh, cover artist Brenton Ceaglske and the balcony people who never stop praying, who never stop loving, who never stop encouraging me...you fill my heart on a daily basis with all that is good. I am so blessed!

All things happen for reasons we may never understand. What I do know is that the glory will always be given to my Creator for all things said and done.

PROLOGUE

One truth will always remain; there are people who come into our lives to just wreak havoc and leave! But then again, others come and leave us with lessons learned and still others remain with us forever.

How our friendships have survived for 40+ years is beyond my wildest imagination. Of course some have embarked on journeys elsewhere; some have come back and reconnected. Some have moved away and some have even died. Yet, for us, this unique group of friends, life goes on. Our families and our businesses are ever expanding. I cannot keep up with all of the changes our little circle has gone through in this life time.

Honestly, I have to level with you. I can't imagine living anywhere but Acorn Hills. I was born here, I grew up here. I did move away to attend college, but moved back because there was this haunting in my very soul. A part of me will always belong here and belong to the value it places on its people and its land. I can't explain it…other than we are connected.

I own the flower shop across the street, Special Occasions. My name is Jillian and I can't wait for you to meet my friends and become a part of our family. Welcome to Acorn Hills. I promise you won't want to leave!

CHAPTER ONE

The town of Acorn Hills nestled snugly at the base of the Cascade Mountain Range with the Klikatka River meandering through the middle of town. It was a community that was booming with businesses; top ranked schools and friendly, welcoming people. The economy was stable. Dairy and fruit farms dotted the land and the citizens, for the most part, took pride in what their town had to offer. The welcome sign at the entrance to the city summed it up well… "Acorn Hills, home of 35,000 amazing residents with a few nuts mixed in for good measure!"

Jake Evans had driven past that sign so many times in his life. Now that he was home again, he'd drive by it a couple times a day, at least. He smiled as he remembered more of why he was back in Acorn Hills.

Living on the East Coast opened Jake's eyes to a lot of differences between the big city and his home town, but now he had to return to Acorn Hills. The death of his father brought him back. Because of that fact, he now not only owned a business but also ran a business; he had a new life to live, new people to meet. And, this would allow him to check up on Jillian Halloran, the woman of his dreams.

Jake's mind had wandered back to the day they had first met. He had taken a few vacation days and had come home to visit his folks. His dad, John, invited him to attend a Chamber of Commerce luncheon and Jillian was also in attendance.

He couldn't take his eyes off of her. From the moment he entered the Oakdale meeting room where the luncheon was held he seemed to watch her every move. There was something so wholesome, so pure and unexplainable about this woman. Jillian Halloran. His dad had told him she owned and operated a floral shop in the new district not far from Austin and Evans. He made a mental note and would definitely have to explore that further.

A car horn blaring behind Jake brought him back to reality. He flipped on the turning signal and rounded the corner to what seemed to be his home away from home these days, Evans Enterprises. He pulled up in the designated "CEO" parking space and just sat there for a moment before grabbing his briefcase to begin the day. He smiled as thoughts of his father ran through his head.

John Evans made a name for himself in the 1970's when he and his partner, Stan Austin, decided to do things "a little differently" in their approach to the business world. Jake was away at college and upon graduation moved to New England taking a job offer from a prestigious marketing corporation. He came home for special occasions and holidays. He kept track of the news and read about the successes of Austin and Evans.

What was once his grandfather's publishing company was now a top notch consulting firm. John Evans took it from Evans Publishing to Austin and Evans, and little by little as time passed, John had the savvy to change and grow the business into the multi-million dollar venture it was today. It was a true force to be reckoned with.

The now three generation-owned business would still provide jobs and financial security to hundreds of citizens in the area. The Evans', including Jake, knew what hard work was and knew that it took teamwork to accomplish things. From its inception, this business gave to the community through scholarships and donations and fundraising.

The community suffered a huge loss when John Evans died. Jake, who was living in New England returned to Acorn Hills for his father's funeral and during the reading of the will found out that he was the heir of his father's shares in the business. And the change began...

After a few months back "in the company", Stan saw that he was no match for the new ideas Jake brought to the table and offered him the option to buy his shares. Stan convinced Jake that he was too old and that Jake had just what it took to bring the company into the future. It didn't take long for Jake to say "yes" and become the sole proprietor and CEO of the company, changing the name to Evans Enterprises.

After the buy-out, most of the furnishings were given to Good Will or to the employees who wanted a piece of the "old" regime. The only thing Jake kept of his father's was the very heavy antique desk. It had belonged to his Grandfather Evans and he had hoped at some point to pass it down to his son or daughter, when and if that ever happened.

The desk was fashioned from the finest cherry that money could buy. The workmanship was impeccable even to the dovetail corners and brass handles. It took a small army to move it from the other side of the building to this location when Jake claimed this spot for his office suite.

It was a beautiful location in the almost all glass building. Jake spared no expense when doing the renovations. He hired the best architects, the best contractors, imported floor coverings and other furnishings. He made sure that comfort was the main word in this project.

Three private suites stocked with wet bars and bathrooms as large as the room was itself were created for visiting businessmen/women; office space was made more than "user friendly" to the point of almost being too comfortable. Jake made his office suite functional as well and again spared no expense. If this business was truly moving into the new century as a success, it needed to look the part as well.

There was a cafeteria that was staffed with an award winning chef, several conference rooms for meetings and a whole floor of this state of the art building was devoted to the health conscious employees. Every kind of work out and exercise equipment was on this floor. Jake had even hired massage therapists and physical therapists.

Behind the building was an arboretum with beautiful blooming trees and plants of every kind and a magnificent fountain in the center. There was a patio for entertaining that had built in grills and wrought iron chairs and matching round glass tables with umbrellas. There was also a roll out canvas that could shelter the entire patio area in case of negative weather elements.

Jake had thought of it all. He wanted Evans Enterprises to be the best…wanted it to look the best, have the best employees, and the best clients worldwide. He wanted his consulting firm to be the one that people asked for by name when they needed his service. Most of all he hoped his father was proud of him for turning Evans Enterprises into the cornerstone of the new business district.

Jake had it ALL; this great business, a beautiful condo that was being custom built to his specs, and the most fabulous girlfriend anyone could ask for. He smiled.

He checked his watch and noticed it was 2:30 p.m. He had spent way too much time "wool gathering". His lunch appointment took longer than he had expected, too, but if it meant he was adding a new client, he would have stayed until dark. Jake was a workaholic. He ate, slept, and dreamt about new clients; how to better serve the ones that were already established and how to make a bigger impact on Acorn Hills and the world in general.

He opened the door to his navy BMW, grabbed the stack of papers on the passenger seat as well as his briefcase and began the short walk to his office. Upon entering the building he greeted the main receptionist and made his way to his work space. Once there he handed the stack of papers to his secretary, Joni, and opened the door to his office. It was time to get started on the next project.

Walking across the room to his desk, he stopped, smiling at what he saw. He was greeted with a warm smile from a woman holding a cup of coffee and a lemon tart. Jillian. He smiled. She always seemed to know exactly what he needed and when he needed it. He took the cup and sack from her and put them on his desk and grabbed her in a head to toe hug, held her tight for several moments then released her.

"Hey, sweet stuff! This is a nice surprise! What did I do to deserve this?" he asked as he peeked into the sack.

"I just thought I'd bring you a treat," Jillian began. "Actually, it has been a horrid day and I just needed a hug from someone who cares." She looked like she could break out in tears at any moment.

Jake hugged her again and just held her. He savored the fragrance of her hair. It was clean, fresh; reminded him of freshly mown grass. Jake took her face in his hands and kissed her passionately. He moved back just enough so that only their foreheads were touching.

"It seems like we never see each other anymore, you know?" she said, looking into his beautiful blue eyes. "With you being so busy here at work and deciding to spend your nights here, too, it doesn't give us much 'us' time."

Jake sighed and caressed her shoulders. "I know, Baby, I know. And, yes, I know work is crazy for the moment. It won't always be this way. There have been so many meetings that have lasted well past 1 a.m. and I just didn't want to wake you up when I came home. You need to rest, too. I know you have been plagued with funerals lately."

Jillian nodded and looked over Jake's shoulder at the assortment of things on his desk. Besides mounds of contracts and file folders, there was a framed photo of her and Jake at the last Citizen of the Year dinner, a crystal paperweight and a note pad by the phone. Jillian's eye read what was on it. "Reservations…Gotham suite…check in 2 p.m. Mmmmm sweet warm Dorian…" She pulled away from him and must have had a really puzzled expression because Jake asked what was wrong.

"What is this all about?" she asked pointing to the note pad.

"Oh, there is a prospective client from Canada that is coming into town in the next couple weeks." Jake explained; his words hurried.

"Care to tell me what 'mmmm sweet, warm Dorian' means?" The tone in Jillian's voice was icy at best. Deep down she had a feeling she KNEW what it was all about but wanted to hear it from his lips, not just assume that she was right.

With a shrug of his shoulders, Jake began, his voice rather nonchalant about it all. "Well, Dorian is someone that has been coming to Acorn Hills for a while now. It is my job to entertain her during her visit. You know how that goes, Baby Doll. I can't say no to a pretty girl." He smiled one of those million dollar smiles and winked at her

"Oh, Jake! First you tell me it is a client that is coming to town. Next you say she has been coming regularly for a while now. Which is it?" She questioned him. Then as if someone had punched her gut Jillian exclaimed with horror and in disbelief. "No! No! Please don't tell me that you have been sleeping with her. Have you been having an affair? Jake, tell me the truth!" Jillian demanded and sat down in the chair that faced Jake's desk.

Jake ran a hand through his hair showing his dislike at her words. He slammed his fist down on the top of his massive desk.

"Oh my God Jillian! You just don't get it!" Jake exclaimed. "Why can't you see that it isn't what you think; you always assume that I don't love you. I DO love you, but I need excitement in my life. You KNOW how easily I get bored. I have needs that just one person cannot satisfy."

He continued, "It has nothing to do with YOU. You are wonderful, but truthfully, it is like eating the same food meal after meal after meal. I get tired of the menu and I want something different." Jake took a deep breath and put his hand on his stomach. Seemed like these days something was always hurting. Eating, breathing, arguing…all of it made the burning in his stomach and pressure in his lungs worse and made it much more uncomfortable for him to breathe. He reached inside is jacket pocket then popped a couple anti-acids.

He rose from the high-backed black leather office chair and walked around his desk to where Jillian sat. She analyzed his every move and stared at him as though what he just said was a scene in a movie, a bad dream. He looked so business-like and so sure of himself. He wore a 3 piece navy Armani suit with a crisp white, wrinkle-free shirt and a tie with navy, silver and light blue swirls. Gold set diamond stud cuff links peeked out from the sleeves of his jacket. His black leather shoes were buffed to a high sheen. His trousers, perfectly creased. The full length windows behind him framed his statuesque figure and made him look even larger and more dashing than he was as he sat on the corner of the desk. He reached his hand forward, and cupped her cheek, his thumb caressing her skin.

"Jillian, Baby Doll, you know I love you. I am not looking for another girlfriend. I have you." Jake flashed a sincere smile. Then he shrugged his shoulders. "I just need to play. It's who I am; and I LIKE who I am. You knew this when we got together. No one woman has ever been able to satisfy me. I love you, but I am just not a one woman man. Sex and love have nothing to do with each other. If we are going to stay together you need to come to terms with this. You need to fix that pretty little head of yours," he suggested as he stroked her hair.

Jake looked at her. Damn, she was beautiful! No other man would maybe see her as he did, but to him she held this wholesomeness that not many women had; especially women over fifty. That in itself was what attracted her to him. She was different than the others that were in his life. Jillian was more of a 'plain Jane' than a striking beauty. She preferred jeans and sweatshirts over designer dresses and heels; yet given the chance, she cleaned up well and could play the part of the society snob almost as well as he could.

Jillian could turn on her charm, flash a smile or bat her lashes and people were sucked into her world...just like he was sucked into her world from day one. Now after three years, she still held his heart, but there was that need to hunt. The feeling of that adrenaline rush was unlike any other feeling. And he hated that Jillian just simply could not understand that. It was just natural human male instinct that made him the way he was. Being with other women was what men were supposed to do.

After all, from before the Victorian era, man's primary job was procreation, and Jake was going to do what he could to hold up that end of his responsibility. Who was he to stop what history had started thousands of years ago? Besides, "hunting" was what he did best and he wasn't too bad at the "kill" either. There was such satisfaction in the release. It was like a lion hunting an antelope; it was a dance and after so long of playing with your food, you finally got to enjoy the feast!

Yet after dining a few times on the same woman, it was time to move on to the next...to find a new food source that would meet his needs to diversify the menu. There were never any strings attached, until he met Jillian. Then it was like his foot was caught in the door...just like Professor Howard Hill with the librarian. Until there was Jillian, all the relationships were meaningless. There was no one to talk to on the level he could with her. There was no one he felt comfortable laughing with; and going out to movies and concerts and business functions together brought him great satisfaction in knowing the woman he was with was probably the smartest in the room. He felt in his very soul that she brought a purpose into his life; but he'd be damned if he was going to change the very core of who he was just for her.

She would either have to put up with his hunting and being with others or be miserable. But, the only bad thing about that was when Jillian was miserable everyone around her shared that joy.

Jillian sighed and shook her head in disbelief at what she had just heard. This afternoon was supposed to be like most of the others. She thought she would be nice and bring Jake coffee and a treat for an afternoon break. And truthfully she needed to see him and needed the physical contact with him. No one hugged her like Jake did and after dealing with wholesalers and customers and orders that went wrong, she really did need the comfort and solace that she felt when his arms surrounded her.

Man was she wrong! Her face reflected the shock of the words that had come from his mouth. How dare he assume that she would be okay with all of this! How dare he say "I love you" in one breath and in the next say "but I need variety"! This just made her blood boil!

Why couldn't he understand that she wanted to have it be like it was in the beginning? Why couldn't he just see how much she loved him and how much she longed to just be the only one he had eyes for? Why was it so difficult for him to admit that what they had was special and better than anything he had ever been a part of? Truthfully, in light of this conversation, she felt Jake was probably doing other women for the entire duration of their relationship. She had given him the benefit of the doubt, but just the thought that there were more made her even angrier. It was too bad she wasn't a witch, because she wouldn't think twice about turning Jake into the blasted belly crawling snake he was being at that moment!

She laughed to herself and she felt a smile cross her face and an eyebrow raise. Maybe becoming a witch and learning how to cast spells wasn't such a bad idea after all. She made a mental note to research spells and creating reptiles from humans.

Jake Evans was THE most handsome, influential man she had ever met. Their courtship was such a whirlwind that she still reeled from the passion when she thought of all the emotions he evoked. At this point, though, she didn't know whether to cry, get angry or just simply ignore him and leave. One thing was certain, Jillian Halloran was a survivor. She WOULD get through this somehow. She just had to.

Jillian pushed Jake's hand away from her cheek. She looked up at him, her liquid amber eyes shooting daggers at the man just inches away from her face. She stood directly in front of him and with every word she spoke her finger repeatedly came in contact with the hardened muscles of his chest.

"Somehow, Jake, I thought I could be enough for you; that was only a part of my mistake." With each word, the poking got more painful because she began using her fingernails instead of the tips of her fingers. She continued, "The other part was falling in love with you so completely that I forgot where I begin."

She took a moment to think about what to say next and then chuckled cynically. "You know, there was a time when I was so addicted to you, so in love with you, so enveloped by your charm," she shook her head, trying to keep from crying. "I honestly don't think you know what love is, Jake! And, you don't seem willing to change or learn either! All I can do now is pity you!

"Damn you, Jake! Damn your need for 'variety' as you put it! What a joke! Jake, how can you not see what you have in front of you? I mean, I know I am not the most beautiful crayon in the box, but I will guarantee you that you will never have anyone else who will love you to the degree I have loved you and cared for you.

"You have been my rock in some very trying times and I have so appreciated that, but that isn't enough to compensate for your latest words and antics. I want to know that I'm important, exceptional; that I mean something to you, that you see me as special. I want to be your only love and I need you and want you to be monogamous. And that word seems to escape your vocabulary, too.

"Frankly, Jake, this what's-in-this-for-me-I-am-number-one-and-I-can-do- whatever-the-hell-I-want attitude just sucks! Well, you know what, go for it! Do whatever you want, and whoever you want when you want. I don't want to be in the back seat Jake, while you are in the front seat with all these other women you find on your travels. I love you and give you all the good parts of who I am only for you to toss them aside for the sake of a different piece of ass whenever you think you need it.

"I don't just want to be normal, Jake. I want to be YOUR normal. But, after what you just said, normal isn't enough and I will never BE enough for you. I have never denied you anything. I gave you all of who I am and it still doesn't seem to be enough."

"But, Baby Doll, you know I love you," Jake interjected as he walked back behind his desk, putting even more space between them.

Jillian wasn't having any of it. She stood up and followed him. She began barking at him again, just inches away from his face.

"I cannot and will not stand by while you charm your way into the beds of other women. You knew how I felt about all this when we agreed you could stay in my home. Now that I know what it is all about I'm not just going to sit idly in the same space with you, not saying anything when you get phone calls and text messages that put this stinking, slimy smile on your face!"

She seldom ever raised her voice, but it was at a decibel right now where those in the outer office could hear every word. She was so angry! A fire-breathing dragon had nothing on her right now. She fingered the Polish crystal paper weight on Jake's desk wondering if she threw it at the window behind Jake just how many shards of glass there would be surrounding them.

She turned around from facing Jake and began walking toward his office door and stopped and turned around to speak again.

"I know what your motives are with these bimbettes, Jake, even though THEY don't. Knowing that you want all of them sexually is more than I can handle. It's like my mind is blowing up with all this crap and you tell me to 'fix my pretty little head?'"

Jillian's voice began trembling. "I'm done, Jake. Do you hear me? I am done!" She emphasized each word. "Come by tonight and get your things. Maybe Dorian or one of your other 'exceptional' women can give you a place to stay until your condo's ready."

She turned and walked towards the door again, then immediately whipped back around. "It has been 3 years now, Jake. Remind me again why your condo isn't ready?" She quizzed him and continued. "I can't and won't put up with this any longer. And truthfully you shouldn't expect me to. Any man who is a REAL man would see the fallacy in your choices. The trust between us has been broken repeatedly.

"So, Jake, tell me, how many other women have you had in the three years we have been together? Was there ever a time where I truly was special to you? Was there ever a time when you said the words 'I love you' to me that you truly meant them? Hell, Jake, trust isn't even in the equation now and I don't deserve this. I'm not putting up with this bullshit any longer.

"You're worse than a politician, Jake, with the double talk. You just tell whoever you're talking to what you think they want to hear. No more smokescreens for me…suddenly the air is amazingly clear and I see you for the slime ball rat bastard you truly are!" Jillian walked back to the leather wing-backed chair where she had been sitting, grabbed her clutch purse and continued walking toward the door.

She threw open the door with such force that it hit the expensive door stop and broke the Italian tile molding that surrounded it. When she slammed the door shut behind her, two of the pictures just inside the door fell to the floor and she heard the shattering glass, but she continued walking out of Jake's office suite and into the hallway.

Joni, Jake's secretary, stood at her desk looking from Jillian's back to Jake's office door wondering what the hell he had done this time.

CHAPTER TWO

There was no doubt Jake Evans was a very handsome man. Standing at 6'2" and 240 lbs., he had a way about him that compared to no one else. His steel blue eyes pierced through you when he spoke, but there was also a softness behind them that not many were privileged to see. His dark brown hair was now peppered with silver, as was his mustache, both signs of his age. For a middle aged man, he still had women falling at his feet, wanting a piece of what he had to offer. It was hard to believe he would be 55 this summer. Fifty plus freaking years old! And just exactly what did he have to show for it? A business filled with incompetent people who didn't know how to take direction or care to put forth the effort to work, an amazing girlfriend, and a high society life style...well, as high society as you could get in this city of 35,000.

He had moved to Acorn Hills after his father, the patriarch of what was now Evans Enterprises, died. A year prior to John's death, Jocelyn, Jake's wife of six months, decided it was time to leave…and leave she did, with the majority of Jake's belongings as well as a hefty sum of alimony! To say the divorce was messy and that it had taken all he had and then some was a definite understatement! At least the business his father had built was not involved in the divorce or she would have ripped that out from under him, too. Thankfully, though, at the time the divorce was happening Jake's father's will wasn't even thought of or written.

The only words to describe Jocelyn were "high maintenance". The daughter of a long-time State Senator, Jocelyn was used to having everything handed to her on a crystal tray. The only thing she had to do was fold her arms and pout and she got her way. Jake found out early on in their relationship that she required "things"…and LOTS of "things". She loved shopping and their 5 bedroom 20 acre estate showed it with the amount of sterling silver; Limoge china, Waterford crystal stemware, and exclusive designer furniture that seemed to take up every square inch of each room. And that was just the tip of the iceberg. There were horses, trainers, groomers, and maintenance people and grounds keepers. Jake didn't care. After all, it was only money and there was only so much one could do with it all anyway.

Jake tried to provide for Jocelyn's every fancy. He hired a fashion designer that was exclusively at her call. He hired a maid, a chef, a personal consultant AND a secretary to manage her "busy" schedule.

He sighed. Just thinking about Jocelyn gave him a headache. She was whiney, demanding and at times just downright rude! He never did figure out what possessed him to marry her.

Looking back on this fiasco, she really was not all that attractive. The way she glared at him and crossed her arms when she thought he would say "no" to her demands made him shiver! She was close to six feet tall with very fine, very straight strawberry blonde hair that reached the middle of her back. Her green eyes were narrow set and her nose reminded him of the stinger on a bee...sharp, pointy.

They'd had the big church wedding with a thousand plus guests at the reception. The whole shindig cost Jake close to a half million dollars; the rental of the cathedral, the fees of the wedding planner and the clergy, the caterer, the cake, the reception venue, the clothing. The flowers alone cost over $35,000.

Then there was the honeymoon in Mazatlan and the trips to Madrid and the French Riviera. Nothing was too good for his bride. Jake shook his head and furrowed his brow at those memories.

As time passed, it became painfully apparent that their marriage was on paper only. She had her own wing of the house and he had his; yet even his room was filled with the treasures she claimed she needed.

As long as he could keep her surrounded with the expensive things she wanted, everything was good. When Jocelyn discovered that he had been with another woman; some business mogul from the Gulf coast, that is when things became testy between them.

He remembered the scenario of the last time he saw his then wife...before the court date. Jocelyn had tossed the entertainment section of the newspaper under his nose as he sipped his morning coffee and asked "what the hell is this all about?" She then, of course, crossed her arms and started tapping her foot on the floor.

The newspaper article in front of him featured a photograph of a plump older woman and he was kissing her. Jake came clean and told her it was as it looked. He had been seeing Devana Morgan for months. At least Devana wanted him sexually which was more than his wife did. He told Jocelyn he couldn't handle being married to someone who didn't want to share his bed.

Jocelyn shed one tear as she walked out of the dining room saying "my lawyer will be in touch." It didn't take long for the attorneys to set the divorce terms and Jocelyn walked out of court smiling broadly at her attorney because of the hefty monthly stipend at the hands of Jake's bank account. And, the possession of all her special "things" that Jake spent hundreds of thousands of dollars on trying to keep her happy.

The job Jake had taken with the consulting firm twenty years ago was an okay job. Yes, it was just okay…nothing spectacular, just okay, and he would be glad to leave it. He had graduated college, married Jocelyn and her father, "the Senator", knew someone who got him the job with the Advent Company in Connecticut.

After the divorce, Jake was forced to take a small furnished apartment. Thankfully he still retained his job. That was the one saving grace and even then it was obvious it was going to take a while to recover from this financial set back!

One afternoon Jake received a call with the news that his father had died. John had been the picture of perfect health most his life. It wasn't until his 70th birthday that he started having issues that required hospitalizations, medications and in home care. He could no longer manage his hectic work schedule and relied more and more on his associates and his partner to pick up his load.

By his mid-70's, John's frail body just didn't want to live any longer. John died the way he wanted, in his home, very peacefully and quietly. The news of his father's death shook Jake to his very core. Jake and his dad never saw eye to eye completely on anything and always had deliberate arguments before ever deciding on a solution. He loved his dad very much but it just seemed that whenever they were together it was a stalemate on all fronts.

Following the reading of John Evans' will it became more and more apparent to Jake that he needed to move back to Acorn Hills. He would assume the helm at the business and start over; new people, new land, new ideas, and hopefully a new life.

Jake's mind continued wandering as he began thinking of what needed to be done with Austin and Evans to make it a fresh, cutting edge company. What was it he could do to bring this company from an archaic, idea ridden mess to a business that made people stand up and notice? He did what he does best, and that was fixing failing businesses.

After assuming the CEO role, Jake took a look at the books and noticed how much money the business was losing because of poor financial management.

Upon this discovery, Jake immediately scheduled time with the Board of Directors and proposed some new ideas, some new concepts that he thought would make a difference. And make a difference it did. Austin and Evans took off and in a few short years this little mundane consulting firm had become a multi-million dollar Fortune 500 Corporation. His father's partner, Stan Austin, could not believe the changes nor did he want to be a part of them at his age, so he proposed that Jake buy him out. With great excitement and relief, Jake did just that.

It wasn't that Jake didn't like Stan because he had much respect for him. It was more that he felt Stan's ideas would hold back the progression of the direction he wanted the company to take.

Jake was finding in his personal life that history was repeating itself, despite his hard work to change his ways. Moving away from Acorn Hills was good for him, but he found upon returning, many of the same people he knew before were still there. And that meant more opportunities to get in trouble, like he did when he ran around on Jocelyn.

Sure, Jake had cheated on Jocelyn, but it was for physical survival. His wife would not even entertain the thought of being in his bed, let alone allow him to touch or kiss her. Enter Devana Morgan. She was available, and more than willing to show him the attention and affection that was so lacking in his life. Devana knew firsthand what he was going through. Her forty year marriage was as much of a joke as his was at only six months. She needed the attention, affection and excitement that Jake needed and so desperately wanted to give it back to someone who would appreciate her efforts. Their affair lasted months before Jocelyn figured it out.

One of Jake's major problems was that he loved women. Not just some women, but ALL women. Sure he knew that he brought it all on himself, but damn it, he just couldn't help how he felt. He loved how they looked, how they smelled. Hell, he could even tell which ones were ripe and in "heat" when walking by them! He loved the curves of full breasts, whether they were a B cup or a double D! He loved the sight of a tight ass as it walked away in front of him; the perfect sway of those hips with each step. Ah, yes, women! His pet word for them was "PITA" which stood for Pains in the Ass.

No two ways about it, Jake WAS charming. He knew how to get what he wanted from just about anyone. He was a master at putting his spin on the truth. People seemed drawn to him like the Pied Piper. Maybe the spin came in a look or in his dazzling smile or in his deep commanding voice. It was different for each situation.

Little did people know that once in his lair, it was hard to get away and more difficult to escape the charming smoke screen that enshrouded the situation. That didn't mean he got off scot free though. Women loved him, men hated him, business associates tolerated him, and others, for the most part, seemed very disappointed in his choices. He let out a breath of exasperation. Life as he knew it.

Jake reflected on the conversation from earlier that afternoon. Jillian had told him to come get his things. Well, it certainly wasn't going to happen right now. He had to think about this; had to plan what was going to be the best for him with this whole thing. His condo was not ready to move into and he really didn't want to spend the money to stay at a hotel. His only choice was to stay at the office. After all, he had spent millions on renovations and it would accommodate his needs for the present time. He would go home and pick up his things in a couple days. He just couldn't do it right now. The reality of those words pierced his heart…Jillian's was no longer his home. It was HER house, her home. He didn't have a "home".

A vision of Jillian plagued his mind. Jillian Halloran wasn't "just another woman"; she had been THE woman in his life for the past 3 years. Jake remembered thinking how "wholesome" she appeared when they met at that Chamber of Commerce luncheon. She wasn't a striking beauty, and in fact Jake would categorize her as "nothing special". But Jillian was definitely bright and funny and caring and compassionate and loving and just simply beautiful from the inside out.

She had extremely expressive eyes, those big, lash-fringed, doe-like eyes that you just couldn't resist. Yet when she was angry her eyes turned to these pools of liquid amber that threw daggers at the opposition. God, he just simply got lost in them every time their eyes met. And, her nose; how he loved her nose…it was just the right size to kiss and suckle. Her breasts fit so well in the palms of his hands; her fragrance, sometimes fruity, sometimes spicy, but always fresh. He fell hard for her the day they met. It was like fireworks and a tilt-a-whirl mixed into one daring ride. Yet, now she was saying it was over? Who was she to call the shots? Who was she to say when it was over? And why couldn't she just deal with the fact that his passion was women?

It was true, yes, he had had several other one night stands during the 3 years they were together, but none of them meant anything. He wasn't "in love" with them, he was "in love" with her. There was a point in his younger days where there would be 3 or 4 a week. Sometimes he would have two dates a day with different women and have sex with them both. He had been with dozens, hell maybe even hundreds of women since college, but he could count on one hand the times he had been in love.

Jake shook his head thinking about it. Pondering this nonsense had giving him a headache the size of Montana. All this romance crap was for the birds. Sure, he could be as romantic as the next guy, but why? He used his charms and "romance" to get his current obsessions in bed, have sex with them; and if they were good enough and there was chemistry between them, they would schedule another time then he could go home. Home. Home was Jillian. Was.

Still staring at the door after her departure, Jake sighed. He was startled from his thoughts by the voice of his secretary announcing he had a call on line one. Quietly he replied, "Thanks, Joni."

"Jake Evans," he spoke into the receiver, his voice deep and authoritative.

"Darling! I thought we agreed you would be at the hotel when I got here? I've been here for over an hour waiting for you, mon chere." The rich, syrupy, Canadian female voice continued. "You do know that I need my Jake fix?" The voice belonged to Dorian Wells-Smithfield, a gorgeous blond heiress Jake met at a dinner party some months back.

They'd struck up a conversation and the next thing he knew they were tearing each other's clothes off in an upstairs bedroom. Oh God, how tight and flexible Dorian was! She was 45, but man did she take care of herself! He loved that about her; that he could bend her any direction and she loved it. Her views sexually were much along the same lines as his. Sex was just for fun, for exercise, certainly nothing with strings. Shit, he didn't even have to get Dorian drunk to take her. She seemed more than willing to just let him have his way and leave. No questions. That is how sex should be, uncomplicated, and certainly nothing to do with love. Love was separate from sex. Granted, there were friendships with those that he bedded, but certainly he didn't love them or fall "in love" with them. More times than not it was just a one-time thing and a phone call if or when they were in the area again.

Jake smiled when he heard Dorian's voice.

"Hiya, Hot Stuff," he replied. "I got tied up. Jillian was here and we had words. She wants me to move out...tonight."

Dorian's cynical, soft laughter tore at his heart. "Well, mon chere, just how long did you think she was going to put up with your philandering? You have to admit, you have done a good job of juggling several women at the same time. But now, now I think it is time for you to figure out exactly what's important to you; better still, WHO is important to you."

"What happens, if I say you are all important to me?" Jake asked with a hint of sarcasm. He smiled devilishly as he thought of being with Dorian.

His phone call was interrupted by Joni's appearance in the doorway. "Jake, the Riley brothers are here and the conference room is ready for your four o'clock meeting." He acknowledged her words by nodding his head and rolling his eyes.

"Listen, Hot Stuff, I have a meeting that I have to attend. Let me get back to you." He tried to hurry her off the phone. But, there was no hurrying Dorian in anything.

"But, Darling, will I see you today? I want you so much, you do know that? And I can't wait to show you what I have been practicing. Picture me..." her voice trailed as she heard the receiver click.

Jake ran his finger around the collar of his shirt. What that woman did to him! He needed a few moments to compose himself to let the imposing hardness against his zipper behave! He knew he was going to have mind blowing sex with a very attractive woman and that thought turned him on so much.

As much as he could sit there daydreaming of what he was going to do to Dorian (more importantly what she was going to do to him), he also knew that there were businessmen in the room across the hall waiting for his words of wisdom concerning their failing businesses. He just wanted the meeting to go smoothly, and quickly, so he could get out of there and change his clothes so he could meet Dorian and relax in her arms.

Before walking out of his office, he checked his hair, made sure his tie was straight and then stopped at his secretary's desk on the way across the hall.

"So, Tiger, is there anything I need to know about this group?" he inquired.

Joni rolled her eyes as she usually did when he called her "Tiger". She couldn't remember when that nonsense began, but it was easier to just roll with it than protest it so that is what she had learned to do.

"No, Boss," she answered. "They just want your expertise to build their business as you have built ours". And with a hearty victory sign she cheered him on.

"Go get 'em!" she raised her eyebrows and chuckled as he winked at her and sauntered across the hall. Jake opened the conference door and greeted his clients as he walked through and began yet another successful project.

CHAPTER THREE

Jillian Halloran walked briskly through the downstairs reception area to the double revolving glass doors, not even bidding the receptionist a good day, as she had the past three years whenever she was at Evans Enterprises.

She knew as she exited with a "bang" from Jake's office, Joni was standing there with her hands on her hips wondering what had just happened. There were other staff members in the outer office as well. She had definitely made her feelings known. She was angry; seeing red angry, but she managed to hold her head high as she flew by them.

With stern intent on her face and the rapid clicking sounds of her shoes hitting the imported Italian floor tile, anyone could see she was a woman on a mission. Right now, her mission was to find her car and get the hell out of here! How dare he! How dare Jake say the things he did to her without any thought about the words he spoke! Diversity? Variety? Really? Oh what a fool she had been!

Jillian had truly believed in her heart, her very soul, every word Jake told her. From the very beginning it was too much like a fairy tale and that should have been a red flag for her to be more cautious. She had promised herself after Brett that she would guard her heart and be more selective with whom she shared herself. Fail…big time! "Well, Jillian", she said to herself, "that worked really well, didn't it?"

All she had to do was walk through the revolving door to be outside and yet she found that difficult, if not impossible. The only thing she wanted to do right now was turn around and go back into Jake's office and slap the shit out of him! Whatever possessed him to go to other women anyway? She could more easily understand it if she had withheld sex from him or was verbally or physically abusive to him.

But in the three years they had been together, she had done nothing but cater to his every need. She brought him meals and drinks when she knew he was working late. She served as hostess at countless business gatherings and used her own business savvy to bring new clients to Evans Enterprises, always making HIM look good. She cooked, cleaned, and consoled. And still he couldn't stay faithful and wasn't even regretful about any of it. THAT is what hurt the most. He cheated and there was no remorse for his actions. It was all in a day's work to him.

Jillian took a deep breath and stepped into the door closest to her and pushed her way outside. Her car was parked only a few feet from the entrance. She hit the "unlock" button on the remote starter on her keychain and climbed into the solace of her five year old snowy white Sebring. Finally… someplace quiet, someplace that was only hers. Someplace without Jake's things, without his voice; without the memory of the words she had just heard. She gripped the steering wheel and began to turn the ignition key but was overwhelmed by what just happened and a flood of tears poured down her cheeks.

She felt empty, angry and hurt by Jake's words. All that he said was like a movie playing in her head over and over again. She just simply didn't get it. How could a man say "I love you" in one breath and in the next be on the phone with someone else making plans for later? How could Jake be so compassionate and caring, caressing her hair and running his finger along her cheek; then in the blink of an eye and with such matter-of-fact tone to his words, go the opposite direction. "I love you, Jillian". "I need variety, Jillian". It was like an endless tennis volley where no one won. Back and forth, back and forth. "I love you. I need variety. I don't want a girlfriend I have you. Dorian is someone I take care of. I love you. I'm not satisfied with just one woman." None of it made sense! Which was it? I love you? Or I need variety?

The shrill ringing of her cell phone brought her back to reality. She silently prayed it was NOT Jake. She used her sleeve to wipe the tears from her face. If it was, she wasn't going to take his call. She just couldn't.

She shielded her phone from the late afternoon sun and looked at the caller ID; feeling a rush of relief when she saw who it was.

"Hello," the word came out so shaky.

"Ju-Ju? Ju-Ju, what's wrong?" It was Ginger. Thank God for someone sane in her life! If anyone could make sense of all this it would be Ginger. Ginger Farnsworth was Jillian's closest friend. They went back as far as she could remember. They grew up within blocks of each other, attended elementary school and Jr. and Sr. High School together and graduated in 1974. They had shared a life time together. They had shared so many "firsts"; so many hopes, dreams, hugs, broken hearts and lost loves. IF there was such a thing as non-blood-relatives-sisterhood, their relationship was its definition.

"Oh God, Ginger! I went to his office. We argued, well, it was actually more me doing the yelling. It was terrible, but I did it. I did it!"

The last words were more powerful than the first.

"I told Jake to come get his things. I can't, I just can't take this anymore. Not after this...not after the words I heard, what I saw on the note pad." Jillian shook her head. "The son-of-a-bitch has been cheating on me. And", she sobbed, tears streaming down her cheeks again. "He has been since we got together. There've been several one night stands. And now there is someone named Dorian. She's from Canada! A client." Her words came out in staccato like sentences.

Jillian knew she was in no condition to drive, but drive is exactly what she wanted to do. Drive as far away from Jake as she could. Drive as far away from Evans Enterprises as possible. Drive as far away from this nightmare that her little car could take her. She didn't want to go home until she was sure he'd retrieved his things and was gone. The last thing she wanted was to see him again and go through all of the painful emotions she was feeling right now. It was bad enough the first time without having to revisit it in the same day. She didn't want to talk with him. She didn't want to listen to any of his excuses. She wanted it done; completely, totally done.

"Ju-Ju, listen to me. Where are you? I am just about ready to leave the shop and I'll come pick you up. We can go sit and have a drink, dinner, whatever you want. You don't have to talk if you don't want to. We can just sit in silence. I just don't want you to be alone. You're in no condition to drive. Ju-Ju, you hear me?"

Ginger was so concerned about her friend at this point she longed for a device that could track where her friend was through the cell phone and magically transport her to the passenger seat of

Jillian's vehicle. Ginger had gone through so much with this woman who was her sister in crime. And now it was her turn to be there, to care for her during HER time of chaos and pain.

"Gin, I'm ok. Really, I am. I'm just leaving Evans parking lot now. Do you want to meet at Turner's? It is only a couple blocks from here. I'm just drained. Maybe you are right. Maybe dinner and a drink will help." Jillian looked in her rearview mirror and turned on her blinker, signaling she was making a right turn and merged into traffic.

"Ok, sweetie, I'll be there in about fifteen minutes. Wait for me, ok?" Ginger pled.

"Yes, Gin. I WILL wait. And, Gin? Thank you so much for always being here for me. I can't believe all the crap we have gone through together. See you soon." Jillian ended the call by pushing a button on her Bluetooth. And knowing Ginger as she did, it would be more like five minutes instead of fifteen!

Jillian opened the sunroof and all the windows and cranked up the radio as loud as she could tolerate. Her Sebring travelled with the flow of the heavy afternoon traffic. Although she could have walked to Turner's, she chose to drive. The gall of some people! Her thoughts turned back to Jake and what he had said to her. "I'm not looking for another girlfriend. I have you."

HA! You only THINK you have me, buddy. Oh, you have no idea what you are in for, you stinking, two timing, belly crawling snake! Karma is a bitch! Jillian continued the line of expletives in her mind. Cussing him out in her head seemed to help. However, as much as it helped, it only brought the anger more to the forefront.

There were so many emotions swirling in her head and if she had to choose just one to describe how she was feeling it would have to be disappointment. It was disappointment in Jake; as a man, as her friend and as her lover. All this time, three damn years of her life, she was looking through rose colored glasses and believing and hanging on every word Jake told her. What a waste! That was time she would never get back.

The one thing Jillian had to do was not look back. She had to stop blaming herself for his narcissistic tendencies. The more she analyzed the conversation they had, the more she saw that it truly didn't matter. He wasn't going to change. She couldn't change him. And somehow she needed to deal with the anger and the love she still felt for him. What an oxymoron!

She tapped the steering wheel in time with the music coming in from the radio. David Bowie wailing "Changes" was playing. Changes. Yes, there would be a lot of them. Thank God there were radio stations that still played tunes she could get lost in! She turned the music up even louder and sang the chorus as loud as she could. She must have really gotten lost in the music because by the time she became aware of her surroundings, she had driven 4 blocks past where she needed to be.

After making sure there was no traffic and against all the rules of her driving logic Jillian did a U-turn and headed back in the direction of her destination. She made a left turn the corner before where she needed to so she could go around the block and be on the right side of the street to park. She may as well have left the car parked at Evans. She shuddered at the thought of the name. As she eased into the space, she noticed that Ginger was parked right in front of her.

Both women got out of their cars at the same time and met half way. Ginger took her in an all-encompassing sister-friend embrace and just stood there holding her while Jillian sobbed into her friend's shoulder. They walked to the bar each with an arm around the other's waist. Jillian tried to wipe the tears from her cheeks before they got to the door. Even though her eyes were red and puffy, she wasn't going to go in there with wet cheeks!

Turner's wasn't just any bar. It was a very nice, upscale place to just sit and talk and unwind after a long day at work. David Turner had purchased what was once a hole-in-the-wall dive and turned it into one of the most frequented after work night spots Acorn Hills offered. He bought the property for next to nothing because it was part of the downtown revitalization plan following major flooding only five years prior.

David Turner, the owner, was no slouch when it came to booze. His many years of drinking, his time in Viet Nam and the counseling afterward changed him from a good for nothing drunk into a very savvy business man. He sure knew what the public wanted when it came to drinks and entertainment and he provided a very safe, posh place to congregate. Beginning at 5 p.m. every week night, catering to the business people who may want to stop on the way home, he served light hors d' oeuvres consisting of a choice of fried veggie baskets or sushi or fresh fruit sticks made from what was in season.

There was live music five nights a week, a tasty varied menu in both food and price, and if Turner's couldn't satisfy your drink needs, there was definitely something wrong! Turner's was known for its ability to create drinks on the spot. The bartenders (drink masters) were top in the country. It was a joy to go to Turner's because you never knew what was going to happen next. The drink masters always had new, synchronized ways of tossing bottles in the air and making the liquid in them land just where they wanted it to. It was like watching Tom Cruise in the movie "Cocktail" only better!

If the bartenders didn't know what you were talking about when you ordered a drink, you were in trouble. The Turner's bartenders each had their specialties, original drinks they created. One of Jillian's favorites was a concoction David himself made from pineapple juice, coconut milk, three different types of rum and a slosh of Grand Marnier. David called that brain-buzzing delight "The Mind Bender".

The décor was elegant, yet comfortable. Some called it "trendy". Some called it "Shabby-Sheik". Tables sat four and were small and square. Some were glass topped with chrome bases, some were all wood with butcher block tops, but all were at a level where you could sit comfortably at them or stand. And they were light enough to push together if there were parties of more than four people. The high backed chairs matched the tables, with their chrome legs or wooden bases and the cushions were all done in a durable ecru colored brocade fabric.

Toward the back of the bar there was a cozy little area with a corner fireplace and some very comfortable overstuffed wing-backed chairs, also covered in an ecru stain resistant fabric with a Baroque design that nicely complimented the other pieces in the bar.

Ginger led Jillian to the back corner by the fireplace where it would be quiet so they could talk, if Jillian wanted. David saw them and came over right away. He embraced Ginger and then saw how upset Jillian was and hugged her as well.

"What's wrong, Ju-Ju?" David pulled away but still grasped Jillian's arms in a comforting and concerned manner.

Before Jillian had the chance to reply, Ginger jumped in.

"It's a day of new beginnings, David." Ginger said. "Ju-Ju's had a terrible day and we need to get her out of this funk. Bring her one of your Mind Bender's please. And I will take a Lime Vodka Collins.

Then, come join us." Ginger looked around and inquired, "Where's Denise? Will she be here after work?"

"I'm so sorry, Ju-Ju. And, yes, Denise will be here shortly. She was restocking some "hot" item at the store." David made quotation marks with his fingers to emphasize the word "hot". "I'll be right back with your drinks." David said and quickly disappeared to the bar.

Jillian couldn't remember how she got the nickname "Ju-Ju" but all her close friends had called her that since high school. Everyone except Richard, that is, who refused and called her "Jilly". And Jake, of course, had always called her "Baby Doll".

Jake. She sighed. Just the thought of his name, the thought of seeing him or hearing him made her physically tremble. She still loved him so much! And this whole thing was just crazy; like some bad nightmare. Only it wasn't. It was reality and it was HER reality. She sure didn't sign up for this part of the relationship! Never in a million years did she think Jake would ever cheat on her. He didn't have any reason to, in her mind, anyway.

Jillian's thoughts were interrupted by the tall, skinny young thing who delivered their drinks and said she would be back soon to take their order. Food wasn't on the list of "to dos" at this point. All she wanted to do was drink and forget what had happened.

All of the words, the looks, the emotions from the afternoon conversation were swimming in her head. How was she to get over this? She HAD to get over it. The sooner the better. Maybe it needed to start right here, right now; a new leaf, a new beginning. Yes, that is just what she needed, a new beginning.

For God's sake she was in her mid-fifties and she was acting like she was still in high school! The only other man who had affected her this much was Brett when they had first started dating. She was so star struck, so enveloped in him, so in love with the feelings of being in love. And all of that was ripped from her, too. Maybe she wasn't supposed to have a happily ever after. Maybe she was only to love unconditionally and when lessons had been learned give it up.

Jillian tipped the glass up and her head back to get the last drop of the first "mind bender" then slammed the glass on the table with a bit more force than she had intended. But the noise didn't faze Jillian. She motioned for one of the bar staff to come over to where they were sitting and ordered another round for them.

Ginger looked at her friend with loving concern when the glass hit the table with that much force. This hurt was different than Brett. It wasn't a physical death, it was an emotional death and Ginger wasn't quite sure what to say or how to handle the whole thing. Jillian definitely needed to get over this and she knew with time it would happen. But for now, how was she going to help her do that? She only knew that she would be there, by her best friend's side, to listen, love and console. Or to just sit in silence as Jillian mourned the loss of the love in her heart for a man who really didn't seem to give a damn.

CHAPTER FOUR

Jake ran a hand through his hair as he listened to this presentation. These morons couldn't find their way out of a wet paper bag! Their stupid freaking ideas made it extremely difficult to keep his mind on the topic at hand, the restructuring of a business to better fit its niche in the corporate world.

His mind wandered. All he could think about was Dorian. All he could see in his head were their sweaty bodies entwined. He began nervously tapping his pencil against his knee instead of on the table, that way no one could hear it or sense his mounting frustration.

Truly, at this point, his business was the last thing he wanted to be thinking about. Only a few short hours ago he broke the heart of the woman he was in love with and yet, despite being upset, there were no tears on her part. What was that all about? Well, maybe she had come to terms with the fact that his needs were different than most. That was a good thing; about damn time!

He remembered her stoic face as he tried to talk sense into her about all of it; then the sound of the door slamming against the door stop when she opened it and the shattering of glass on her way out. Jake was sure that would be the subject of plenty of whispered office talk throughout the rest of the week. He glanced at his watch. This meeting was taking forever! It was now well after five o'clock and he needed food. He needed to just get out of this hell hole. He needed Dorian.

With the final words of his presentation, Jake suggested the client take into advisement the changes on the table before proceeding. He bid his new potential colleagues a hasty goodbye and escaped to his office, leaving the aftermath of the meeting for Joni to deal with. He was done with this for the day. Once behind the doors of this massive suite, Jake removed his shoes and tie. Now he could breathe…for a moment anyway. He had been spending more and more time at the office lately rather than at Jillian's.

After becoming sole owner of the business and changing its name, Jake decided that it needed a facelift. If they were going to be competitive, they needed to look like they wanted to win every account that walked through the door. He designed the interior of the office complex with several private shower suites for visiting clients from other countries. His private suite was larger than the other and it was there just in case he couldn't get away, just in case meetings ran longer than normal and he didn't want to drive across town. He smiled. If the truth be known, the real reason he installed a private suite was for those "just in case" moments; those outside chances for a "nooner" or "quickie". He raised an eyebrow, and gave an evil grin and chuckled. Yes, he liked who he was and what he had become. After all, this WAS his world.

Jake grabbed the phone receiver and looked in his directory. He quickly found Dorian's cell phone number. After a few rings a soft French Canadian accent sounded on the other end…"Hello".

"Hey, Hot Stuff! I am just leaving the office. I think we need to meet at Turner's for drinks and a bite to eat. Then we can go to your place and you can show me those new moves you teased me with earlier," he said in that sexy, low tone that was uniquely Jake.

"Darling, I will be ready in ten minutes. I will meet you there," and with a click, Dorian was gone.

Jake headed for the shower to hopefully wash away the tension of the afternoon. The water was hot and pelted hard against his taut muscles. It felt wonderful and he could feel his neck and shoulders relax. As the water surrounded him and he relaxed more, inhaling and exhaling the hot steam, his mind replayed scenes from the past.

Jillian would stand behind him most nights when he came home. She would soap his back and then massage those muscle knots in his shoulders and neck until they were gone. She usually led him to their bedroom and continued working on his tension which left him in a relaxed puddle on their bed, or heated up for some damn good sex!

He shook his head. No time to think of such things now. It was evident that she was done with his, how did she say it? "Bullshit". He chuckled out loud and again shook his head at how she acted. She'll come around, he thought. And if she doesn't, oh well. He knew there were many others who wanted him. That was the beauty of having so many women to wander to, all of them wanted him. But with that each woman seemed to attach to him and eventually "fall in love" with him. That wasn't his problem. He was not responsible for their feelings or how they reacted to his interaction with them. He could guarantee there would be no strings this time…none; at least on his part.

He turned off the water and slid open the glass door, reaching for the towel before his feet hit the black plush rug in front of the shower. He continued drying off then secured the towel around his hips. As he passed the full length mirrors he took stock in what he saw; a very handsome, very fit, and yet still aging man. He looked closer, noticing there were some unruly mustache hairs. He took the scissors from the counter and clipped them, reached for the bottle of expensive French cologne and splashed some on his face and torso then walked to his closet. He knew the one he chose was Dorian's favorite. That would win him brownie points.

It was a warm late afternoon. He decided on a pair of white chinos and a lime green golf tee. Because of the heat and because he just didn't want to he decided to forgo socks and slipped on the pair of light tan Dockers that were sitting by the foot of the dressing settee where he sat. He stood, fastened his belt after tucking in his shirt, ran a brush through his hair, flossed his teeth and out the door he went, ready for the evening of "fun".

The reception area was empty except for the janitorial service. He nodded to the person mopping the expensive imported tile floor and started whistling as he exited the building. His Mercedes convertible was parked just outside the door and to the left in the lot that was designated for employees. Climbing behind the steering wheel, he made sure the top was down and set out for Turner's. He really enjoyed that place. Since its opening, they had received many awards. It was just a nice spot to go for a drink. It wasn't filled with moronic business types or young entrepreneurs or kids. It was HIS kind of place.

Dorian said ten minutes. He checked his watch. He should have walked, but he drove, just so he had a way back from Dorian's hotel. He arrived at the bar, checked his hair in the rearview mirror, put the top up on the car, locked the doors and shoved the keys in his pocket, keeping his hands hidden comfortably as he walked into the bar.

The coolness hit him as he opened the door and walked in. He scanned the room and saw many colleagues and nodded acknowledgment before he took a stool at the bar and ordered a martini; very dry, no olive. He downed the delicious liquid in two gulps and ordered another. He sighed. The light jazz background music helped relax him and that was a good thing. It seemed like he needed it more than he originally thought. He was half way through the second drink when he felt the heat from the open door behind him. Looking up, he saw Dorian and immediately could feel his body respond at the very sight of her.

Dorian was a strikingly beautiful woman. She was 45 years young with the body of a teenager. Her long blonde hair was pulled up into a tight, high pony tail but still fell past the middle of her back. Her manicured nails were polished with a fuchsia nail color and her fingers laden with so much "ice", it was a wonder that her hands weren't frost bit! Even in this light the diamonds sparkled from her wrists and fingers! She wore a cute little hot pink sundress with bows on the shoulders. She took off the over-sized sunglasses as she entered the bar and immediately spotted Jake. She slowly walked over to where he was and gave him a long, passionate kiss, sending chills through him.

"Hello, Darling," the sultry words were enough to pulse what was already hardened and waiting!

"Dorian", Jake smiled, putting his arm around her waist. "It is so good to see you. What a helluva day it's been." He returned her kiss with one that made every nerve in her body sizzle. Dorian ran her long slender fingers through Jake's hair, down his cheek to the sensitive spot on his neck. "Darling, leave everything to me. I promise you by the end of tonight you will not remember anything about today." She kissed him again and took the stool next to his. She crossed her long slender legs at the knee which made her dress climb up even higher. Jake's sharp intake of air was proof he noticed her deliberateness in teasing him. He turned his attention to the bar tender and ordered another martini and a Manhattan and the appetizer tray. As he looked from the bartender to Dorian, out of the corner of his eye, he spotted her…Jillian.

Jillian was sitting in the back corner. Her animated movements and frustrated expression was evidence of her mood. She was very upset and Jake knew that he was more than likely the topic of THAT conversation!

Hell! When was this going to end? His first instinct was to run to her and find out what was wrong, comfort her, but he didn't. He didn't want to always be looking over his shoulder, always walking on eggshells, always wondering when or if she would find out if he was with someone or what he was doing.

Jake also knew that if she saw him with another woman it would crush her. He really didn't want to hurt her. He truly didn't, but, he wasn't going to give up the life HE wanted either. No chains. HA! Even though she hadn't put chains on him, they were there. And because of that at times he felt like that bird in a gilded cage. He felt obligated to be with her, to care for her. After all, he loved her. Didn't he?

His hand found the soft skin of Dorian's neck and he lightly massaged it as he thought about his life and what lay ahead. Dorian softly sighed at his touch and leaned into it more.

"Oh, Darling," she leaned into him and whispered into his ear, her breath warm, tantalizing, "what you do to me!" She looked up into his passion filled eyes. She grabbed his hand and gracefully slid down from the bar stool. "Come, let's go." Her sultry voice did things to him none other could.

Jake downed the last swallow of his drink and tossed enough cash on the counter to cover the food he had ordered but hadn't eaten. Hopefully someone at the bar would eat it so it wouldn't go to waste. He took Dorian's hand and led her out of the bar. Dorian handed Jake the keys to the rented vehicle. He opened her door and helped her in then got behind the wheel and closed the door.

Jake felt himself getting hard at the thought of what she had planned. To just tear her clothes off, see that supple, flexible body, taste those hard nipples, see her perform for him. O God! That brought shudders through his entire body as he thought about how she would feel under his touch. He revved the engine, checked the mirrors and peeled away from the curb.

Even in the car on the way to her hotel, he couldn't keep his hands off of her. She was so willing to let him explore every inch of her body, mind and soul. The first was definitely what he wanted at the moment. His hands massaged her thighs, wandering up higher to that soft warm mound that would receive him later without hesitation. She moaned his name softly and that turned him on all the more. By the time they got to the hotel and he got out of the car it was nearly impossible to hide that strong, hard growth rubbing against his zipper, making it a challenge to even walk.

Dorian gave Jake the key to her suite and he unlocked the door. He tossed the keys on the end table by the couch, kicked the door shut and immediately took Dorian in his arms and kissed her as clothing landed here and there, strewn across the room. Somehow they made it to the couch, tumbling down on the cushions still kissing and fondling one another. Jake bent his head and took one of her nipples into his mouth, running his tongue over it again and again bringing it to a hard peak. Dorian arched her back so that she was pressing her breast more into his mouth. She loved how he felt against her body, loved the warmth of his breath on her skin. Her breathing was so labored from his touch. One of his hands caressed the other breast and played with the hard nub while his tongue continued to flick fire on the one in his mouth.

"Jake, oh, Jake" she sighed. She gently shoved him off of her and took his hand so he would follow her. She went over to the pile of pillows by the fireplace and knelt before him, her hands running up and down the toned muscles of his thighs.

Jake stood in front of her, his hands in her hair drawing her closer to his hardened shaft that was waiting impatiently to plunge inside of her. She licked the underside of his shaft, sending shudders through him. She took great delight in what was before her. She took his hardness in her mouth and toyed with every inch, running her tongue back and forth in gentle small circles that made his pulsing more evident. Feeling what she was doing to him, her tongue found the very tip of him and she teased even more.

Jake could barely contain himself. He knew at any moment he would certainly explode! He stopped her actions as he moved lower and lower until he was kneeling on the pillows with her. His mouth crushed hers with a searing kiss. He trailed light kisses down her neck, between her breasts, his tongue leaving a fiery trail behind.

They continued this heated dance. He held Dorian's hands so she couldn't touch him. Her staggered breathing and occasional "Jake, oh Jake" gelled in his mind that she liked what he was doing.

His hands released her wrists and he gently pushed her back on the pile of pillows. His fingers searched wantonly until he found her soft folds. He parted her then dipped his head, placing gentle kisses here and there until his lips found her hardened bud that was screaming for more of him.

He gently rubbed his tongue over her, bringing her to even a higher dimension, to the edge of that cliff. Just as she felt she could handle no more, she begged him to take her. And take her is just what he did. He held her hips as she brought her feet to his shoulders then he drove deeply into her. She held tightly onto his hands as she enjoyed the repeated waves of pleasure she felt with Jake moving in and out of her. She screamed his name just as he filled her with his warmth. His breathing labored, her body glistening with perspiration. It was over as soon as it began. Deed completed. Check!

She wasn't one for snuggling or physical contact afterward. She just simply wanted sex and wanted him to leave. Pretty simple. So, he did just that. He walked into the bathroom, took a towel and cleaned himself off a bit, got dressed and left. After the day he had he really wanted to jump in the shower with Dorian and feel the sleekness of her body under his hands as they soaped each other, but that would have to wait for the next time, he guessed.

It certainly wouldn't take much for him to want to experience her all over again. Yes, a shower, then bending her over while in there and caressing her breasts as he entered her from behind.

Dorian tied the belt of her red silk robe and followed Jake to the door.

"Mmmmmm, Dorian, what you do to me!" Jake exclaimed breathlessly then passionately burned a kiss into her mouth. She finished the kiss and then quickly shooed him out the door. There was no good bye or we'll talk soon. No words exchanged. Uncomplicated. Just the way he wanted.

Jake made his way down the hall to the elevator that would take him to the main door of the hotel. He really wished it could have continued through the night. He wanted to hold her and be held and fall asleep only to wake up and go at it again.

The elevator doors opened and Jake walked toward the front desk and then to the door. He bid the doorman a good night and stepped outside. The coolness of the night felt good after all that activity.

Dorian's hotel was only a few blocks from where his car was and the walk felt good. Maybe it would clear out his head. He noticed as he walked that his shortness of breath got worse. He would schedule a doctor's appointment when he got to his office in the morning. Wait, he was staying at the office from now on until the condo was ready. He checked his watch. It was already after midnight and Jillian would absolutely kill him if he showed up at her house at this hour!

He made his way back to the bar to pick up his car and go the few blocks back to Evans Enterprises before he collapsed on the couch for yet another night. He looked down at the sidewalk as he continued walking, still troubled by the events of the day. He had parked around the corner from the front of Turner's. And as he turned the corner, he ran smack into someone, his hands instinctively reaching out so as to not knock the other person over.

"Will you watch where you are going?" He asked angrily.

He lifted his head, shocked at who stood in front of him. He breathlessly spoke one word, "Jillian!"

CHAPTER FIVE

Richard's Relics was THE antique shop of the Tri-state area. People were spreading the word about the "incredible quality of fine antiques" that was housed in this building which encompassed one full city block.

The circa 1800 brick building had a charm all its own. For being as old as it was, the building still maintained its original charm; inside as well as outside. Decorative brick cornices crowned each of the large beveled glass windows on all three floors. Stained-glass half-moon panes took up residence under the arches and told the story of the early years of this historic city, scene by glorious scene.

The building was divided into several showrooms on every floor, each with its own theme. One had nothing but pre-Civil War furniture and memorabilia. The next displayed beautiful porcelain china ranging from Limoges to Royal Rudolstadt to R.S. Prussia and pieces from well-known pottery moguls Hull and McCoy; and even some early matte-finished Wedgewood.

In every room on every floor, dressers with beveled oval mirrors, oak four-poster bed frames, and cherry buffets and étagères lined the walls. The third floor was home to time piece jewelry and vintage clothing, complete with an office for alterations. And, the most amazing thing of all was that these items all sold like grits in a Southern restaurant! Richard Dempsey had truly made a name for himself. The store had become what only business owners could dream of; successful!

Richard had lived in Acorn Hills his entire life, all 61 years of it. He attended school, proudly served his country through two tours of duty in Vietnam as a Special Ops Navy Seal. Thankfully he returned home unscathed; physically, anyway. His family was so proud of their only son. So when it came time to "settle down", as his mother called it, Acorn Hills was his choice.

After a few months of getting his feet back on solid ground, he decided maybe a degree in "something" might be a good idea. The G.I. Bill paid for his education at Coral Knoll Community College and after graduation hired him on as the V.A. counselor for students who, like him, were transitioning back into society after serving in Nam.

It was a great job for him. He truly enjoyed being the one to help steer these men and women into the new phases of their lives. He retired from that position twenty years after beginning it. The world was different and there was little need for "war counseling".

Because his parents were getting up there in age, Richard chose to stay in his childhood home. He made sure his mom and dad were taken care of physically, emotionally and financially. He led a fairly simple life; work, church, family; the three most important things in his world. Most of the people he had gone to school with were busy with their own stuff…families, work, whatever, so there wasn't much socializing. Many of his buddies had left Acorn Hills and some had even died serving in the military right by his side.

He saw no need for a serious relationship at this point in his life. Living with his parents had not been easy for him. His mother, now 85 and his dad 88 were both relatively healthy for their age but with the added responsibilities of their care and trying to figure out his own place in life after leaving the college, the white-picket-fence-two-and-a-half-kids-dog-and-beautiful-wife dream was just that, a dream. It was a bittersweet thought that was tucked way back in the darkest corner of his brain. Sure, at some point he was certain it would happen. But, for now, it was low on his priority list.

Fourteen years ago when the Braxtons retired and decided to sell their antique business, they encouraged Richard to consider buying it. Richard had always had a passion for old things and had dabbled in woodworking as a young man in high school and in his parents' garage on the weekends.

He remembered how each wood had a different smell, grain pattern, a different feel; and Richard loved how the varieties took on personalities as he worked with them. He loved the smell of fresh sawed oak, the smokiness of it, that pleasant, almost forest perfume from cedar.

It didn't take Richard long to give Roy his answer. After a resounding "yes, hell yes!" he and Roy Braxton shook on it and that "contract" was good enough for Roy. Richard remembered Roy and Penny were fixtures in Acorn Hills, had been there since he was a youngster. They were highly respected and Richard was proud to own what Roy and Penny had devoted their lives to. He remembered the store always smelled like a combination of all the woods it held and of rose water, the fragrance Penny wore. Roy was a tall thin man with very little hair and glasses and Penny was almost as tall and skinny as a rail. When you looked at the couple you were reminded of the Grant Wood painting "American Gothic". Richard shuddered, minus the creepy overtones, of course! He never had liked that painting because of the looks on the subjects' faces.

Richard was a devoted student, hard worker and always passionate about "getting better"; but never in his wildest dreams had he imagined this business could turn such a profit! While in college for a business degree, he also took some classes in antique artifacts, just for fun. He seemed to have an eye for what to purchase and what to stay away from.

When the papers were signed and Braxtons was legally his, their sign came down and a new one replaced it. It was now known as Richard's Relics. In the short time he had owned it, he was able to pay off all of the outstanding debt; not only for himself but also for his sister Stephanie, and his parents, as well as providing the money for their funerals and burials.

And with all that done, he could still live comfortably and be able to stick a good amount in savings for that "rainy day". Although, at his age, he wasn't sure about that day at all, or if he would even live to see it.

Richard, now 61, was still unmarried with no heirs, no children to carry on the Dempsey name. So, when he thought of where all of his assets were going when he died, the only ones he could think of were his nieces and their children. His sister, Stephanie, was 2 yrs. older than him and had severe heart issues. Her three daughters were all married with children of their own, and Richard was certain they could use the money from the sales of the assets. He sighed. This was something to think about another time, not now.

Why he was in this maudlin mood was beyond his comprehension. Richard continued to play over in his head all of the things that had gone on after the purchase of his store.

David Turner had approached him 2 years ago with the idea of putting in a "trendy" bar down the street. Richard had concerns about the whole thing. He and David had spent time together in Nam and he just wasn't too sure how that would work and he really didn't want to see David fail. It was a foreign concept; not fitting in at all with his antique store and the other shops in this corner of town. He and David had discussed the pros and cons and left it with Richard telling David "do what you think is best."

It turned out to be the "best" for David and for the rest of the shops that were so worried about what the connotation of having a "bar" in this area would be. But after the bar had been up and running and David decided to be open for lunch for the "business crowd", Richard saw an increase in walk-in traffic, especially from business men and women looking for that extra piece for home, or that gift for an upcoming client or anniversary. This was especially true in the summer months and during the holidays. It indeed proved to be an absolutely tremendous idea and he supported David now 100%.

David and Richard were in the same graduating class. They knew "of" each other, but it wasn't until enlistment day that they began this brotherhood friendship. Richard was the star athlete and David preferred art and music. On the day of deployment, Richard noticed David walking onto the bus that carried them out of town. They had been through a lot together, both putting their lives on the line for their country.

When they arrived back in Acorn Hills, David just couldn't settle down. The habits he picked up in Nam, mainly the use of marijuana , made it difficult for him to focus on anything, so he left for California the same day Richard enrolled in classes at CKCC. David was following his dream of being a "roadie". He and Richard had had many conversations in those jungle bunkers about following rock bands and how cool it would be to have no responsibilities.

David's dream ended when he was arrested for possession of marijuana. He served his time, kicked his habit and returned to Acorn Hills and floated from factory job to factory job.

He found that he enjoyed the taste of alcohol as much as he did weed and he began thinking. He could attend bartending classes at the local community college and start a business. Richard and David reconnected at Coral Knoll and shared a few beers now and then, but became closer after Turner's opened. David purchased the antique oak bar that Richard had in his store and this began a strong relationship that they both decided should have begun a long time ago.

Shortly after Turner's opened, David had brought Denise, the love of his life, into Richard's Relics. She was opening her own shop several doors down from his and hoping she could find furnishings that would appropriately display her merchandise.

Richard had secretly hoped that David and his sister Stephanie would take their relationship to the next level, but it never happened. Stephanie found a stuffed-shirt accountant to marry and David stayed the party boy. Richard smiled and shook his head as he remembered his reaction to the conversation the three of them had that day.

"So, Denise, what is the name of your business?", Richard asked, hoping to get a handle on just what type of display items and or furnishings she would need for what she was selling. If he didn't have it, he knew where to get it and would go the extra mile for his customers on all levels.

Denise smiled and her eyes twinkled, as she bit her lip and looked at David, who smiled this cheesy grin and gave her hand a reassuring squeeze. "Sultry Sensations" she softly answered, almost in an embarrassed tone, blushing as she spoke the words.

Richard's left eyebrow raised and a smirky expression crossed his face. "Ummmmm, what exactly are you going to be displaying?" By this time,

HIS face was beet red just thinking of the possibilities.

"Well", Denise began, "It is a very upscale, tasteful adult pleasure shop for women…"

David broke in "She sells sex toys, Richard. All shapes…and sizes…and colors."

Denise smacked him hard on the arm. "What?" David chuckled so loud that it resounded in the chambers of the store. He rubbed his arm where the hand of his lovely lady made contact with him. "That hurt", he said, still laughing.

"I don't just sell toys, David, and you know it!" Denise glared lovingly at David and continued on. "I have books, imported lingerie and many other items that enhance a woman's romantic and sensual experience." she proudly stated noticing that Richard's face was still red.

Denise knew it was an unconventional business, especially for the snooty community of Acorn Hills, but she knew it was all going to work out…hopefully. She spent hours meditating, lighting candles, invoking angels of protection and finances and business. It had to all be okay, yet with the history she had in this town it was debatable. All she could do was try her best.

Being from the "wrong side" of the tracks was a strike against her. She spent all of her growing up years living in the shadows of the skeletons in her family closet and all of her adult years trying to prove herself to those around her. They soon would find out that she was a savvy business woman and could bring revenue into this community, but she had to convince them to believe in her. Small towns created so many uphill battles. And even though Acorn Hills was NOT that small, there were areas that were as clicky as Junior High School girls!

She smiled and continued, "So, what do you suggest, Richard? What can I use to showcase my items?"

Richard chuckled at the memories of leading Denise and David around the different show rooms and Denise choosing this and that and grinning from ear to ear with what Richard suggested. He remembered, too, that as they were walking around making decisions Jillian popped in "just to say hi". She often did that just to check up on Richard. It became a daily routine. Sometimes it happened more than one time a day, depending on what was going on in her world.

Jillian and Richard had been friends forever. There was never anything romantic between them, but it seemed they had always had each other's backs from the time they met, even though back then she was in first grade and he was in fourth. He remembered how cute this precocious little girl who lived next door was and became very protective of her. That aspect of their friendship still remained. It was mutual.

Even though they were apart during Richard's stint in the service and

Jillian's years at college and marriage, they finally touched base again when Richard bought the building for his store. It was like they'd never been apart at all. Jillian was President of the Acorn Hills Chamber of Commerce and on the welcoming committee for new businesses when Richard first opened. Her business, Special Occasions, a full service floral shop was across the street nestled between the bakery/catering shop and the new coffee house.

So, when she wasn't busy, she often stopped at the bakery and then to get coffee and headed across the street for conversation and to make sure her best friend was doing alright. She had always been able to bounce things off Richard and he did the same. They likened their relationship to something similar to 'Will and Grace' and sometimes 'Felix and Oscar' of television fame. He enjoyed the banter with Jillian and looked forward to her visits that had become a welcome routine.

Richard rang up another sale for the day, and put the credit card receipt in the cash drawer before he closed the register. He made delivery arrangements with the customer for his team to take the precious grandmother clock to its new home, thanked the customer, and began whistling. He looked at the register tape in disbelief.

Today alone he had taken in over ten grand! He glanced at his grandfather clock when it began chiming and noticed it was well past 6 pm. This clock sat in the corner of his grandparents' home and he remembered how fascinated he was when he was a little boy and he heard its' chimes. He was so honored when he was notified after his grandfather's will reading that he would be the new owner of it.

It was once again time to close for another day. Richard smiled and counted the day's activities, recorded the deposit, turned out the main lights and made his way to the front door, flipping the "open" sign to "closed". The doors at Richard's Relics were locked until 10 a.m. tomorrow. He was different from the other stores on the strip. He decided to open later in the morning and remain open after most of the residents of Acorn Hills got off work. It seemed to work well as evidenced by today's sales.

With the deposit in one hand and the other hand in his pocket, he walked down the street whistling. He smiled. He had begun whistling in Nam when the children would have such fright on their faces from the sounds and scenes in front of them. He lost count of how many he taught to whistle and how much bubble gum he handed out in the time he was there. Funny what you remember and how some things just continue to haunt you regardless of how much you try to make them go away.

He shook his head. Yes, life was good at this moment. He was heading to the bank and then over to Turner's for a beer. Not only did he deserve that, but a cold one would taste amazing after a day like today.

CHAPTER SIX

The way those infamous 'Mind Benders' were going down you'd have thought Jillian was drinking water. She really did enjoy the taste of a good alcoholic beverage, especially on days like today; but normally she was not a drinker. Sure she did her fair share of drinking right out of high school, just like most of her friends. The legal age for drinking back then was 18 and when she turned 18 a group of her friends grabbed her by the hand and took her bar-hopping.

Her very first drink was a Lime Vodka Collins. It was pretty watered down and she really didn't see what the big deal was about drinking. It came in a tall slender frosted glass with a couple maraschino cherries. After the fifth one, she gave up and began trying to tie knots in the cherry stems with her tongue. Even that, back then, didn't seem all that difficult. On subsequent "hopping" outings, she wet her palate with sloe gin, rum and cola, Jack and cola, tequila. If it was booze she'd drink it, everything but vodka, that is. Her lifelong friendship with alcohol was off to a roaring start.

And surprisingly enough, she'd had only one hangover in her entire drinking career, and it wasn't even associated with her high school or college days. It was with a co-worker and it was a huge mistake at that. One hangover, compared to those her friends usually bragged about, was truly something for HER to brag about. She gave a heavy sigh and turned her attention back to what Ginger was babbling about.

"You know, Ju-Ju, you need to just forget about that asshole and all the things he has done to you. This has been going on for months now, no, probably from the beginning of your relationship, and frankly, I'm tired of how Jake has been treating you. You deserve so much better. He is such a slime ball!"

Ginger took a sip of her Tia Maria and ginger ale before continuing. "You certainly don't deserve someone who is going to be so damned disrespectful of who you are and what you stand for. Honey, there is no way, no way in hell I would put up with my man seeing and screwing other women. No way!" She put the glass back down on the table and signaled for another round.

"Ginger, we've been through all this before," Jillian shifted in the chair so she was facing her best friend. "In my head I KNOW what a jerk Jake is, tell my heart that!" She covered the center part of her chest with both hands.

"I can't just turn off the feelings I have for him. I truly am, oh hell...I mean I WAS in love with him. Well, maybe I still have some of those feelings for him, but I have to face the writing on the wall. He will never change until God strikes him with a bolt of lightning and even then he would argue with the Almighty that he was the one who was right!"

Jillian closed her eyes. She was not going to cry. She was not going to be so upset as to raise her voice in public just to deal with her feelings. She took a deep breath to calm the hurricane that seemed to be brewing inside her. After opening her eyes she reached for the glass in front of her and took a larger gulp than she had intended. "I will not be played by him or anyone else." She emphasized each word as she said them.

"You know, the more I think about this, Gin, the more I see signs that this has been going on for longer than just the last few weeks." A puzzled look crossed her face and she continued.

"He has issues. I mean real, deep issues. He uses people in any way he feels like as long as it helps him out and he doesn't see any problem with it. He is always right," Jillian pounded her index finger on the table "and everyone else is wrong." She looked around at the throng of people taking seats around them and lowered her voice, although she didn't know why. She truly didn't care what anyone thought of Mr. Jake Evans.

"And the saddest part of all this is that he will never ever take responsibility for his actions! After all, he hasn't done anything wrong." She mocked. "So in his mind, this means that if someone is hurt, it is THAT person's problem." Another hefty gulp slid down her throat.

"He's used me for the last time, Gin. You know, when we first started dating, I'd heard stories of how he was such a womanizer. But, and you know this better than anyone, I actually thought when we became an item, he would want to change; that I would be enough for him.

"But, seriously, Gin, I don't think any woman will ever be enough for Jake Evans, ya know?" Jillian drained the bluish green liquid from the glass and reached for the one that was just delivered, plucked the pineapple slice off the rim and began eating it.

Ginger grabbed hold of Jillian's hand, nearly knocking the drinks over, "Oh, honey," she was nearly to tears, the alcohol evidently affecting her a lot more than it was her friend. "I know how you must be hurting. But I also know that this is for the best." She patted Jillian's hand. "I know it really hurts right now, but in time you WILL be okay." She reassuringly said. "Trust me."

Jillian downed the drink she was holding in record time and with gusto set her almost empty glass back on the glass topped table, the clink loud enough to make some customers' heads turn in their direction. Yes she knew "in time" all of this would be behind her. But right now, it hurt. It hurt way down to the depths of her very soul. There was a hard pit in her stomach every time she even thought about him and the way her chest hurt at every little thing that reminded her of "them"... all of it just brought back how hard "right now" was going to be, how much it was going to hurt...for a while.

How dare he think he could do this to her or to anyone, for that matter! From day one, she knew she was in trouble with Jake. No one had ever made her feel fireworks just by looking at her and smiling. Jake did that. No one ever showed her such tenderness and such assurance in her as a person and as a sexual partner. Jake did that. Yet, there was always this nagging feeling in the back of her mind that she just didn't quite measure up.

Now, she knew why. Now she knew that she would never and could never be enough for Jake. It was not her fault, even Jake said that. She wasn't the reason that caused him to be this way. He was this way when they met and hooked up. There was always going to be a skirt that turned his head; if not today, certainly this week; if not this week, then this month. It didn't seem to matter...age, size, shape, he was a cad when it came to women. It took a long time, but it was a good thing that she was finally seeing him for his true colors. Discovering his want for women and his narcissistic God's-gift-to-women attitude made her want to hurl!

Jillian raised her arm and signaled the bartender for another round of drinks for her and Ginger. As her hand went into the air, it was captured from behind in mid wave. Jillian turned around only to find her friend, Richard Dempsey, standing behind her with a huge grin plastered on his face. He bent down and kissed her on the cheek and moved across to the other side of the low table and did the same to Ginger.

The three of them had been summertime friends who did everything together. Richard was graduating high school as Ginger and Jillian were beginning. He was the star athlete during his high school days. He could do no wrong, but unlike some others at that age, he never let it get to his head; he was never anything less than a kind gentleman. There were still many trophies in the cases at the school heralding his accomplishments. Jillian was fortunate enough to have lived next door to him. Growing up her brother and Richard were good friends.

"Hiya, Jilly, Ginger." He pulled another over stuffed wing back chair over next to Jillian and sat down. Richard smiled and said, "Okay, what's a guy gotta do to get a beer around here?"

Jillian waved her hand again and summoned the waiter. Half way there she loudly requested "bring my friend a Killian's and another round for us", she gestured to Ginger and herself.

She knew she'd already reached and surpassed her drink limit, but at this point, she really didn't give a damn. The more immune to this bullshit she could become, the better it would be. It hopefully would kill the last little iota of feeling she had in the dark corners of her heart or, if nothing else, at least make this one day easier. She could already feel the steel cage beginning to form around it and it felt cold and dead. More booze, she thought, more booze will make it better. She tilted her head back to get the last drop from the last drink.

"So, Richard, how's business?" Ginger asked, as a Killian's hit the table from the bar server who seemed to disappear as fast as the drinks appeared.

"I've been so busy, kinda feel like a cat in a room of rocking chairs," Richard chuckled, taking a long, slow pull from the bottle now before him, thoroughly enjoying the swallow as it went down his throat.

"Well, I guess that is good then, huh?" Jillian remarked.

"So, Jilly, what is going on? I've never seen you drink this much before." He eyed the eight empty glasses on the table, six of them were hers plus the one in her hand. He had a worried, puzzled look that was unsettling to her.

She turned her eyes to her drink and began stirring it with her finger. She could never hide anything from Richard, damn it! He always knew when something was bothering her, always. That was the mark of a true friend; knowing when something was wrong without having to say a word.

"Let's just say it is liberation day", Ginger replied clearing her throat.

"I see," Richard began. "This wouldn't have anything to do with Jake the Snake would it?" he directed his comment to Jillian who had just finished drink number 7.

"Yesh, Richard, it has everything to do with him, but I really don't want to ruin my mood by discus-hing it now." Her words slurred now when she spoke. "Please, can we schpeak about someting else? Lovely weather, huh?" She batted her eyes at him and smiled.

Richard laughed. He knew when Jillian said she didn't want to talk about "things" she really didn't want to talk about it. However, at some point, he also knew that he'd either get a phone call or an email requesting him to "come over". And he'd go to her place with a pint of double chocolate brownie ice cream and two spoons and spend the rest of the evening listening to her try to justify her actions.

Jillian had used Richard's shoulder many times in the past to plead her case or to vent about failed relationships. Among those many times were Brett's untimely death, how to deal with two growing male teen-agers, the death of her parents, or just something that upset her or brought her joy. Richard had rejoiced with her when she decided right out of college to start her own business, a flower shop. He had just returned from Viet Nam and had even offered to invest in it, but she wouldn't hear of that.

    She was a very confident, independent woman. He admired those qualities in Jillian. He remembered when she and Brett Halloran (his high school football nemesis) were married. He thought it was one marriage that could withstand just about anything. She had two small children and was running her own business. Everything was going so well. Richard had called Brett to see if he still wanted to meet for racquetball but there was no answer. He called the flower shop and one of Jillian's staff had informed him that Brett was in a severe auto accident that morning and was pronounced dead on arrival at the hospital.

    After that devastating news Richard found he became even more protective of her and the boys. All he could remember was the shock on her face when he walked into the hospital and the boys sitting with their grandmothers and other family members.

    To lighten the conversation and keep from talking about "things" Jillian didn't want to at that point, they spent the next half hour or so discussing the local sports teams, the new businesses that seemed to be popping up everywhere, and the success of their own businesses, including the one they were patronizing, Turner's. Ginger suggested that they order some appetizers for dinner and another round of drinks and they did just that.

    "It is exciting to see the new growth to our town, don't you think?" Jillian asked of the other two.

    Richard was the first to agree with her and then Ginger, totally schnockered at this point, added her views of it.

    "Who'd have thought back in the 70's that Acorn Hills would be this hub of action; this center for foreign and domestic businesses?" Richard drained his second beer.

    "I just remember how much fun we had back then. We didn't have to worry about locking our cars or our houses. We could walk to the store or to get ice cream after school and not worry about being mugged. I'm not so sure I would try doing that today." Jillian added. By this time her mind was really feeling "bent" from the drinks she had downed so quickly without eating.

    Ginger took another bite of the mozzarella stick she'd been nibbling on and affirmatively shook her head. "Yes, it was so much more simple back then, so uncomplicated."

    Uncomplicated. The word rolled in Jillian's head. That was what their relationship was to have been, uncomplicated. She and Jake were to continue doing what they were doing; loving each other, being there for each other. He wasn't supposed to "complicate" this...this...this whatever it was. Yet, it was complicated now. Her emotions were complicated now. Her life was complicated now.

Jillian held another drink in her hands and just listened at Richard and Ginger laughed and went down memory lane with more stories from football games or math class or summer touch football games in the Dempsey's back yard.

Two hours had passed as they shared stories about high school and past relationships. Richard looked at his watch.

"Well, girls, I hate to break this up, but I need to get going. I still have some things to take care of before I hit the sack. It has been a joy spending so much time with you two. I miss you guys. We need to do this more often." He touched Jillian's arm "You do know where you can find me if you need me, right?"

His sensitivity brought a tear to her eye. She knew if she continued down this trail of thought she would be sobbing again. Making light of the conversation, she assured him she would phone him later and explain everything, but only after she'd had time to process it all.

Richard touched her cheek, his hand so warm and reassuring. There was an unspoken response from each of them as their eyes met. He stood up and stretched, reached across and fluffed Ginger's hair and smiled again at Jillian before he left. Richard knew before tomorrow was over, Jillian would phone him so he made a mental note to stop at the store for the double chocolate brownie get- me-out-of-this-funk ice cream.

"Ju-Ju?" Ginger began, touching her arm to get her attention. "I think we need to get moving too. It's nearly midnight and we both have to work tomorrow. I'll walk back with you to where you're parked. Are you sure you're okay?"

"Gin quit worrying! I'm okay. I'm shtrong and a survivor, remember?" Jillian laughed at how silly her words sounded then briefly hugged her dearest friend. If she lingered, tears would certainly flow and she just didn't deserve to be so sad right now. They linked arms and walked out of the security of Turner's into the night air.

It was a beautiful evening, perfect for a walk. And after all the alcohol she'd consumed breathing some fresh, cool air felt really good. Jillian was wishing the apartment above the shop was finished so she could just go a few blocks and up some stairs and be home. Instead, she was walking a couple blocks to her car. She and Ginger turned the corner and headed for their vehicles.

Jillian had to admit she was maybe just a wee bit light headed after all those drinks and sure that the morning would bring even more "mind bending" but, she smiled, thinking how good they tasted. It had been a long time since she and Ginger had been out drinking. Now she knew why…even though she loved the drinks, she wasn't as young as she used to be and the alcohol was hitting her harder than she remembered.

Neither she nor Ginger paid much attention to anything but the conversation they were having and Jillian was trying her damnedest not to walk like a drunk. And in her attempt to do that she ran smack into someone or something. She would have landed on the pavement if it hadn't been for the strong hands on each of her upper arms. The touch, grip felt familiar. She looked up and sighed. "Jake" she softly uttered.

CHAPTER SEVEN

The events of the day, more so of the evening, haunted Ginger as she walked up the steps to her home. No lights were on so she wondered if Jordan was even there; truly hoping he would be because she needed just to be enveloped in one of his all-consuming hugs.

The security lights came on just as she put her key in the lock and opened the door. Closing the door behind her she kicked her shoes off in opposite directions almost immediately as she entered the foyer. She glanced through the mail on the black Sonoma rectangular table just inside the door and grabbed what was probably important. She hung her purse over the coat closet door knob and continued walking into the great room.

Sasha, lovingly referred to as "Monster Cat", greeted her with the customary meow and I-love-you-my-human-give-me-something-to-eat rub against her ankle. Ginger stooped over and picked up the long haired tortoise shell cat, cradled her against her shoulder giving her the attention she demanded.

"Hello? Honey, you here? Did you feed Monster Cat?" she called into the dark.

"In here," a voice came from down the hall. "And yes, she's been fed. She's just playing you for treats. Be strong." He chuckled, knowing one of Ginger's weaknesses was that damn cat!

Jordan Everling sat at a desk in the cozy, dimly lit den working on some kind of paperwork. The fireplace was stoked and gave a warm, comforting glow to the corner opposite of where he sat. He raised his head and pushed the designer black plastic-rimmed glasses back up his nose.

Just as Ginger entered the room, Sasha jumped from her arms, landing on the overstuffed chair by the fireplace. The cat settled and began washing her paws; her tail encircled her and she passively looked up at them as if to say, "be quiet I am going to take a nap."

Ginger walked over and tenderly kissed Jordan on the lips. She smiled. Even at one o'clock in the morning, he was still the most handsome man. She didn't know how he could pull that off, especially since she looked like something Sasha drug in from outside!

Jordan's jet black hair was never mussed and his mustache and pencil beard were always perfectly groomed. The chestnut heather colored turtleneck smelled musky, smelled like Jordan. She lingered, closed her eyes and drank in his scent. There was something so calming about him. For a man in his mid-50's he still looked fabulous, at least to her, and that was all that mattered! She so loved this man!

"Oh, Jordan", she sighed and shook her head. "You just wouldn't believe what's been going on today!" Ginger continued, "You know, first it is the nonsense at work then tonight. I just feel so sad." She tossed the mail she'd carried into the room with her on the end table by the chair where Sasha perched, hoping she remembered to retrieve it before heading to bed.

Jordan pulled her onto his lap, encircling her within his arms. "You're home now. Sit here with me." He softly urged, "Put your head on my shoulder and de-stress for a few moments. Then you can tell me about it if you want."

He noted the heavy smell of alcohol on her so he knew this was going to be a good story if she could tell it before she passed out. She was already yawning against his chest.

Ginger and Jordan had been together, off and on, for 15 years. Jordan asked her to move in with him the same day her parents moved from their house to one of the new condos. They both figured it would be good so as to save money. While that sounded like a logical reason, it was truly because he was selfish and wanted to see more of her. He had planned on asking her to marry him, there just never seemed to be a right time, though. Their busy lives didn't lend much time for "togetherness" and Jordan thought by living in the same space at least they could have the going to sleep and the waking up time together.

Ginger was top in her home economics class in high school and went right into culinary school after graduation. Her dream had always been to own and operate her own catering business. She dabbled in it from the time she was 16 years old, when the company hired to provide food for the annual National Honor Society event somehow forgot!

She and the Home Ec. teacher put their heads together and came up with what turned out to be the best banquet the school had ever hosted. From that night on, Ginger was the go-to-gal for catering parties or other events. Teachers, parents, and students phoned Ginger requesting her help. Soon she saw that her hobby had become her passion and she was quickly outgrowing her parents' kitchen and moved into the family garage.

She put the business on hold while she was at culinary school. Once she returned to Acorn Hills, her phone didn't stop ringing with requests for her to cater and/or plan parties and banquets and weddings. Everyone seemed to know she was there, thanks to the big mouthed mother she had! The orders increased weekly and that is when she knew she needed to do something more permanent if she was ever going to keep doing what she was doing.

Ginger's father suggested that she look into buying a building in the ever growing down town area. When the small storefront next to Special Occasions, Jillian's floral shop, was for sale, Ginger saw the opportunity and she jumped on it. She was now the owner of a building and a business she'd named 'Mystic Capers'. She offered a full catering service as well as some of the most delicious baked goods Acorn Hills had to offer. The display cases were usually sold out by 10:30 a.m. People sometimes stood in line to make sure they purchased their daily "fix" of sweets from Ginger's shop.

On her 40th birthday Charles and Kathleen took their daughter to an art exhibit at the Pavilion in Coral Knoll. It was where she met Jordan. He was looking over some of the art, but kept one eye on her as well. They exchanged chit chat and Jordan handed her a business card and told her he'd be in touch because his employer had been looking for a catering business for their client parties.

Kathleen Farnsworth was not too pleased about this strange man talking with her daughter and when it happened again at the farmer's market, she truly didn't know what to think. But after getting to know Jordan she saw there was something special between him and Ginger. So long as he treated her lass well, all would be just fine.

Jordan helped the Farnsworth's with their packing and moving. It all seemed like such a blur now to Ginger; the move, the award, the changes at Mystic Capers, the wedding. And all she saw was Jordan folding his arms and smiling at her as she tried to soak it all in.

She certainly had her work cut out for her, especially with this bomb about Jake that Jillian tossed her way, but she had the strength to take it on. She would be there for her friend regardless. She smiled and closed her eyes, savoring the fragrance on Jordan's sweater.

There were so many areas of her life that were going so right. She really did love Jordan. She truly always had, from the first time she set eyes on him. She remembered how their eyes seemed to lock onto each other from across the room at the Pavilion. He said "hello" and that was all it took.

As she sat on his lap with her head on his shoulder, Ginger breathed a sigh of relief. She was home. Finally home. She had left the house at six this morning, dealt with cranky so-not-morning workers, soothed the feathers of worried mothers of brides, assured businessmen their luncheons were the most important things on her calendar, and then there was the Jake drama with Jillian. Ginger traced Jordan's beard line with her index finger.

"Jordan, I am so worried about Jillian."

"Why is that, Pumpkin?" he massaged her shoulder with one hand and held her waist with the other. He softly placed a kiss on her nose.

"Ju-Ju told Jake to get out. She was so upset. In the years I have known her; I have never seen her so upset. After the day I'd had, I called her to see if she wanted to meet for drinks at Turner's. She was sobbing so hard I could barely understand her." Ginger shifted her weight so she could see Jordan's face as they talked.

"I was wondering when things were going to come to a head, Ginger." Jordan confessed. "This has been brewing for months now. You can't expect a woman to put up with her partner flirting with other women and actively having other sexual encounters. Ging, there is no way I could ever think of doing something like this to you, or anyone else for that matter. Only a coward and an immature…well, ass would do anything like that."

Jordan made a very good point. This wasn't right on so many levels. Ginger was just glad Jillian had finally seen the problems with it all. She appreciated Jordan's frankness with the subject. And her heart was warmed by the words that he would never entertain even thinking of doing what Jake was doing. No woman in her right mind would put up with this garbage. And, Jillian deserved so much better. She deserved the love and attention of someone who really truly cared just for her.

"Jordan? You knew Jake was snaking around?" She asked.

"Pumpkin, how long have we been together? How many functions have the four of us attended together? I saw how he looked at other women, always winking, always that smarmy smile and raised eyebrow. It wasn't hard to figure out."

"I suppose you're right." Ginger continued, "We wound up meeting at Turner's for a couple drinks and to talk this thing out. I have never seen Ju-Ju drink so much! She had eight Mind Benders. Eight!" she held up eight fingers. "And the strange part of it all was I don't think it even affected her one little bit, until the end when Richard left. She was slurring her words some."

Jordan chuckled and took Ginger's left hand in his, fingering the emerald on her ring finger. "So, two very attractive women, sitting in a bar, getting blitzed with another man." He raised an eyebrow and affirmatively nodded his head. "Wow, if I didn't know Richard, I'd be jealous!"

Ginger rolled her eyes at Jordan's comment, knowing he was trying to cheer her up a little while still showing he cared.

"Thankfully, Ju-Ju had gone to the rest room when Jake and one of his bimbettes were at the bar. I was so tempted to go over there and give him a piece of my mind!" Ginger's voice raised in strength as her hand formed a fist. "I am so upset with that...that...that snake!"

"Pumpkin, try to calm down" Jordan urged, massaging the small of her back.

"She's my friend, Jordan, and she's hurting, damn it! I'm just glad she told him to get out. Richard Dempsey was there, too, and he joined us. Sorry, I think I already said that." She apologized. "I think that really helped Ju-Ju. I know he's seen her through so much in the past. Maybe he can get her through this as well."

Jordan sat straighter in his chair and grabbed her shoulders and pushed her back a bit so he could see her face. "Now, don't you go playing Ms. Matchmaker here," Jordan cautioned. The seriousness of his voice and the amount of alcohol she consumed made her want to laugh, but she knew better!

"The last thing Jillian should be thinking about is another man in her life. These times hurt and right now she needs to deal with all this bullshit and heal from it on her own before complicating her life with another man."

He looked her in the eye. "You, my little pumpkin, just let things take a natural road." He touched the tip of her nose with his index finger. "Gin, if Richard is meant to be in Jillian's life things will progress, and they will progress without YOUR meddling." He kissed her cheek and drew her closer to him which put her head back on his shoulder.

"Well, I know you are right, but I just want her happy and if Richard is the key to that happiness...I'm just sayin'. She shrugged. "And, I have always had this feeling that they'd be together at some point in time," her voice trailed off for a moment as she got lost in her old reflections; remembering the countless times they were all together and how she thought even back in college days Jillian would wind up with Richard.

"The funny part of this whole thing was when we left. Richard left first, thankfully. We finished our drinks, and then we left. Had Richard witnessed what happened next, he would have beaten Jake to a bloody pulp!

"Jillian and I were laughing and talking and not really paying attention to anything around us. As we rounded the corner to our cars...BAM! She walked straight into Jake! I don't know which of them was more surprised."

"Oh my God, Gin! You ARE kidding, right?" Jordan sat up so quickly he almost dumped Ginger on the floor. He began laughing. "I'm surprised I didn't get a call for bail money because the two of you beat the shit out of Jake!"

"Well, I didn't stick around. I know I should have, but frankly I was and am totally exhausted. With the day I had and the booze, I really didn't want to deal with any confrontation. There didn't seem to be any shouting between them, so maybe all it turned out being was a "bumping into" one another and they went their separate ways." Ginger said, her voice betraying that she was second guessing her earlier actions.

Ginger shrugged her shoulders. "However, knowing Jake as I do, I can't imagine there not being any strong words exchanged between them. And I know that Jake was to have gotten his things out of Jillian's place tonight, but I highly doubt that happened since we didn't leave the bar until after midnight." Ginger yawned.

"These are matters to worry about at another time." Jordan eased her from his lap and stood up in front of her with his arms still encircling her. He lovingly placed a hand on Ginger's cheek. "You do look tired, Pumpkin. I'll tell you what, how bout we take a nice hot shower, and I give you a massage to work out the kinks of the day?"

He tenderly kissed her lips. "I love you, Gin," he declared, with such passion in his voice. Ginger could feel herself melt at his declaration and she felt entranced as he looked into her eyes and passionately kissed her again, lingering longer this time.

Jordan scooped her up into his strong arms and carried her to their bedroom. Ginger put her arms around his neck and softly giggled at him carrying her. She flicked off lights with her toes as they walked down the hall.

Yes, she liked the sound of letting the day's troubles wash down the drain. And what wouldn't go that way would surely leave as soon as those tight muscles in her back and shoulders were kneaded. And Ginger was fairly sure, if the last kiss was any indication of what else would happen, her tension would definitely be gone following the hot sex she and Jordan would share.

She smiled against his chest. Oh, yeah, she was not as tired as she looked or as tired as Jordan perceived! He was in for a treat, but from what she was feeling against her as they walked down the hall, so was she!

CHAPTER EIGHT

Two weeks had passed since that fateful running-into-one-another scenario outside Turner's. That was so totally unexpected; the literal running into Jillian, but more so the feelings that were again brought to the surface.

Damn! Damn it all to hell! Jake remembered how beautiful Jillian looked just standing there, looking at him like a deer in the headlights of an oncoming car.

Electricity shot from his hands through his arms straight to his heart when he braced her so she wouldn't fall. She ALWAYS affected him that way; made him feel like he was standing under a tin awning in a lightning storm. There was just something about her; her energy, her smile, just her! All that reached way down in his soul and attached itself like a cocklebur.

Jake shuddered remembering the feelings that moment evoked. That's when he knew, in his gut, that he had quite possibly lost the best thing that had ever happened to him, the best thing in his life, really. Jillian truly had been the only woman he had ever been in love with, but her restrictions made it impossible to live together. He closed his eyes briefly. It was too late, he couldn't think of all that now.

He had gathered his things from Jillian's the day after she requested and brought them all to his office. He had chosen a time when he knew she would be at work so he didn't have to deal with confrontation or the feelings he still had for her. It hurt him. Those words, her tears, knowing he had hurt Jillian; yet hurting in the inner most part of his being like he'd never hurt before. He lost a part of himself and there wasn't a damn thing he could do about it.

He removed the boxes he'd packed and kissed the key before laying it on the kitchen table. Jake turned out the lights and closed the locked door, never again having access to Jillian or what he had called home the past three years.

Since that day, Jake had been sleeping on the couch in his office. The nights were fitful with dreams of Jillian and Dorian and work and other things. Despite his best efforts to just forget it all, on most nights sleep evaded him.

Jake knew he needed to get up. Today was another day and it wasn't a light one; it was a day filled with meetings and an overseas flight to secure yet another business venture.

He stretched his arms over his head and there were audible crackles as his body protested his movements. When he finally rose from the expensive leather couch, the covers tangled around him and Jake banged his shin against the sharp corner of the coffee table and his toes wrapped around the table's leg. "Fuck! Damn that hurt!" he muttered as he limped the entire way to the bathroom. Certainly the hot water would help. It couldn't hurt, anyway.

His clothes from the day before fell behind him, one piece at a time. He stepped over the tile edge of the shower and reached for the faucet. He turned the knob; setting it as hot as he could stand then slowly adjusting it higher and higher until he had created his own personal sauna. He stood under the pelting spray for close to 30 minutes before finally deciding it was enough.

Thankful no one arrived early at his office, Jake strutted naked across the plush carpet to the massive closet. He marveled at the selection before him. That portion of the closet held more Armani suits than most department stores could claim. He chose a heather gray three-piece and light pink shirt that already had a tie draped around the hook of the hanger. The shirt he chose, of course, required cuff links. He wasn't going to take the time to go through all of them, so just picked up the ones from yesterday, the diamond and gold squares. That was followed by picking up the pair of black leather shoes at the end of the couch, which he buffed the scuffs out of.

As he passed the mirror, he took stock of how he looked. Jake shook his head. He was getting older, and this morning was one of the few times it really showed. Or maybe it always showed and it was the first he noticed. His hair was more silver at the temples, the worry lines in his forehead and around his eyes were deeper, and his demeanor was not happy or carefree any more. The corners of his mouth were even down turned. The joy was gone from his spirit, his life and he just looked tired, old; angry.

Jake sighed. Checking his teeth after flossing, he used the mouthwash, sloshed on one of the expensive colognes that lined the counter then leisurely sauntered out the door of his private suite. The massive cherry doors closed behind him and he found himself standing in front of his desk. It was business as usual. There were clients who were depending on him to bail them out or buy them out or just give his wisdom to them. It all came at a hefty price though. Jake Evans never gave anything away, unless it was himself.

I can't be bothered with such trivial thoughts as aging, he thought. After all he had a company to run, a business to buy, a woman to, well, womanize! He chuckled. And yet today he felt like shit. He couldn't stop coughing; the shower hadn't completely loosened up his stiff neck nor had it taken the pain out of his bruised shin and toes.

There was a pressure in his abdomen that hadn't been there before this morning. The thought of an overseas flight later tonight sent him over the edge. He reached in his jacket pocket and popped a couple antacids. Today would be an interesting day, to say the least.

Jake checked his desk calendar. The first meeting of the day was scheduled at 9:30 a.m. He still had 20 minutes to gather his thoughts. Jake walked around his desk and sat in the high backed leather chair, reached forward and thumbed through the address spinner sitting on his desk, picked up the phone and punched in numbers.

"Hiya, Cupcake!" Jake smiled as he swiveled in his chair. The "cupcake" he was referring to this time was Sindra Austin, the 19 year old daughter of his ex-business partner, Stan. "I haven't heard from you in a couple weeks and I just wanted to check up on you," Jake continued with a slight hint of concern in his voice. Yet the sly smile and twinkle in his eye revealed his "concern" had an ulterior motive, like normal. Jake always had an ulterior motive where women were concerned; that being to get them into bed as fast as he could.

Stan approached Jake about putting his daughter to work last summer after graduation. The office needed extra clerical help. Joni had planned to be with her daughter for the birth of her first grandchild and Sindra was available, so to keep her out of trouble and give her the chance to earn some money would Jake be kind enough to consider offering her a job. Well, of course he did, how could he tell Stan no. Besides, she was a very attractive young lady, and after seeing the clerical skills she had, Jake used her as Joni's replacement. He and Sindra developed quite the friendship that summer.

Sindra was your typical 19 year old; immature in some ways, very mature in others. She spoke her mind. She had the most incredible ice blue eyes and she was such a flirt! Someone right up Jake's alley! Her age did not matter to him, and it took little time for Jake to befriend her. Soon they were calling one another several times a week and meeting for shopping outings, dinners and concerts.

Jake was so taken by this young lady. She made him laugh. She made him feel young again, and there certainly was nothing wrong with that! When fall came, Sindra left for college in Coral Knoll, a suburb of Acorn Hills. Jake went to Coral Knoll several times that fall and winter to spend time with Sindra. He kind of felt sorry for the poor kid. She didn't have many friends in Acorn Hills and hadn't made many at college either. Sindra's parents offered little support so she attached herself to Jake because she was so starved for attention.

Jake became Sindra's sounding post. They talked about everything from school to work to relationships, even sex. Jake smiled as he remembered some of those wee hours of the early morning conversations. The one thing that still evaded him was getting her into bed. But that time would come soon enough. They'd certainly talked enough about exploring that. Jake assured her that he would never hurt her and that if she wanted to experiment with different sexual aspects, he would be available to teach her what he could.

"Jakey!" Jake could feel the smile and vibrancy coming from the other end of the phone as he heard Sindra's bubbly words. "I have missed you so much! It's so boring here. Can you come for a visit?"

Jake's smile widened. He was hoping for just that type of a response. "Of course I can, Cupcake. When?"

"I have class until 3, but free after that." The excitement just dripped from every word she spoke.

"How 'bout we go to dinner around 6-ish? I can't wait to see you. I have missed those baby blues of yours," Jake admitted.

He made a fist and pulled it toward him and mouthed "yes". This would be the day he would have little Ms. Sindra Austin eating out of his hand, or eating something else. He wiggled his eyebrows in a sinister move.

"Wear something that is going to show off that beautiful cleavage of yours, Cupcake." Jake teased. "I have to go…have a meeting…counting the minutes until six."

"Can't wait to see you either, Jakey" Sindra rang off and he could almost see her dancing as she put her cell phone in her pocket. He could see her voluptuous melon-sized breasts bouncing…just that thought alone made him hard and got his mind off the worries and frustrations of that morning.

Jake stood and straightened his tie before picking up the folders on the corner of his desk. Yes, distractions would be good right now.

"Good morning," he nodded as he passed Joni's desk and proceeded to Conference Room 1 where the Board of Directors sat. This was going to be a long morning. There were decisions to be made and a lot to discuss about the overseas expansion of Evans Enterprise holdings.

Joni followed him into the room, files in one arm a pen in her mouth and a coffee cup in each hand. She sat one steaming mug down on the table in front of where her boss sat. "My, you're in a good mood this morning." She whispered to him. Joni made her way to the other side of the table to her designated spot where she put the other cup of coffee and the stack of folders.

"Good morning everyone," Jake began. "The sooner we get started, the sooner we can get outta here." He smiled and everyone chuckled and papers began to shuffle.

Part way through the meeting, Jake had a horrendous coughing spell that wouldn't subside, and he quickly excused himself before running toward the restroom. It took a while for him to recover this time. He wasn't quite sure what brought these annoying attacks on, but after Japan, he would see his doctor. It was probably nothing, just stress or a virus that would pass, but better to get checked out and be certain. He returned to the Conference Room with a smile, quick apology, and jumped back in without missing a beat.

Three hours later the door opened and handshakes were given. As soon as everyone left, Jake poured another cup of coffee, sat back down in the same spot and put his feet up on the desk. Now, just how in the hell was he going to accomplish what they wanted him to do?

Even though he was CEO and owner, he respected those he had chosen to be on his Board of Directors. He knew they held the best interest of his company and he also knew he could trust each of them with all Evans had to offer.

Flying to Japan later tonight to secure the purchase of Tomeiki Ltd., signing papers, etc., Jake sighed and shook his head. Just what he needed…another project. However, because of his position, he WAS the right choice to send to do the bidding and the buck did stop with him. This was a great opportunity. Acquiring Tomeiki would seal the corner on the Asian market. He knew he had to follow through. He couldn't send someone else to Japan for something as important as this. This was a big endeavor and a lot of people here and abroad were counting on him to get this done, and done right.

"Joni," he shouted, forgoing the intercom because the meeting room door was still open. "Clear my schedule tomorrow and for the rest of the week. I will be leaving for Japan later tonight. I don't expect that it will take more than a couple days, but I just want to make sure I don't miss anything on this end. Just handle what you can. Go ahead and book the hotel for a week and if there are changes, I'll call and you can do whatever you need to. I know Bruce has the company jet ready to go so if you could make sure all of the other files are in order for me to take, I'd appreciate it."

Joni ran across the hall in answer of his beckoning.

"Yes, Mr. Evans. Is there anything else?" She inquired checking the yellow note pad that had become a part of her daily attire.

"No Tiger. Just hold things together like you always do in my absence." Jake winked at her and continued putting stacks of papers into his briefcase.

It was nearly 1 p.m. and Jake was getting hungry. He ran downstairs and grabbed a sandwich and cup of soup from the cafeteria on the main floor. He savored the first bite. It really tasted good to have food, and he could feel his energy levels and mood rising. He realized that it had been a couple days since he had eaten. That was probably why he wasn't feeling too well.

His mind wandered to the phone conversation he had prior to the meeting. Sindra. He sighed and took another bite of the turkey sandwich. Sindra, the little minx! He laughed out loud. Yes, it was definitely going to be an interesting afternoon and early evening. Shame he would have to cut it short to head off to Japan because he just knew there was going to be great enjoyment taking what Sindra was offering him.

Jake and Sindra had many conversations of the "what could be" of being together sexually. She was unlike any he'd met, making her riper for his picking! She was not afraid of being hurt. In fact, she said she rather enjoyed inflicted pain during sex. It was, how did she put it, "Exhilarating." And, that was a part of his psyche that he really wanted to explore and, well, since she was so willing, why not?

Certainly this was going to be a great experience for both of them. He would make sure of that. This curiosity of one another was something that was just bubbling from the beginning of seeing/meeting each another. The first day he saw Sindra in that low cut tight sweater and those leggings and heels Jake knew he had to have her. Just the sight of her turned him on and it became more and more difficult on a daily basis to hide exactly what she did to him.

Yes, he was looking forward to this rendezvous later; the possibility of dominating this young thing and making her submissive to what he wanted her to do. He would never hurt her. He couldn't do that, but the things that were running through his mind at this point made him wish her hands were on him right now.

This was a moment to just completely let go and satisfy his curiosity; not to mention satisfy whatever Sindra wanted to try. There was no way Dorian would be submissive to him like Sindra seemed to want to because she always had to be in control. And God knows, Jillian, miss vanilla ice cream with no sprinkles, would never in a million years even entertain the thoughts of something like what he would try later today. He may never have an opportunity like this one for quite some time and he may as well make the most of it…right? He tried to justify it in his own mind and took a look at his watch.

He could ponder such things later, because right now Jake needed to toss his lunch trash and get back upstairs for the next meeting, after controlling yet another round of coughing.

CHAPTER NINE

Five o'clock had finally arrived! Glad for the afternoon to be at an end, Jake changed into jeans and a light blue polo for the amusing endeavors of the evening. He donned his sunglasses and headed out the revolving front door of Evans Enterprises…receiving good night wishes from other employees or just smiles from the females with him winking in return of their appreciation. One thing was certain Jake Evans made a statement wherever he went, even in his own company. Heads turned and smiles happened whenever he passed by.

Jake slid into his Mercedes and opened the sunroof, checking his hair in the rearview mirror. Sure, it was a bad habit, but there was nothing wrong with wanting to look good. The only problem was after the roof slid open the sun revealed even more silver in his hair!

He eased out of the parking lot and merged into traffic. The drive to Coral Knoll was beautiful during this time of day. The late afternoon sun felt wonderful as it beamed through the open roof of the Mercedes. It was only a 20 minute drive from his office to Sindra's front door. He usually couldn't get away until about this time of day, so because of the afternoon 'going home' traffic, Jake always chose the back roads and this one was one of the most beautiful in the city.

This road followed the river and was lined with many different types of trees. Late spring/early summer in Acorn Hills and the Pacific Northwest, in general, was spectacular! The flowering almond trees were in bloom with bright lavender flowers; dogwood, magnolias, rhododendron and azaleas were showing color; tulips and daffodils were vibrant everywhere. The city recognized the beauty of this route. It was dotted with multiple parks with plenty of benches and play areas, including dog parks.

There was a convenience store on the way so Jake stopped to top of the tank and grabbed a bottle of water. He also took a bunch of flowers from the bucket on the counter, paid for his purchases and continued on his journey.

Sindra only lived two blocks off this main road in an apartment with three other students. It didn't seem to take Jake as long as it normally did to get there, or maybe he was just lost in thought. Before he knew it he was in the driveway and had turned off the car. Tossing his sunglasses on the passenger seat, he grabbed the bundle of flowers and made his way up to the door of her apartment.

Sindra evidently had been watching for him because even before he knocked on the door, it opened. She stood before him in tight, very short cut- off jeans and a canary yellow tank top that was (quite intentional, Jake was sure) two sizes too small. Sindra was well built for a 19 year old girl. Her legs were short and very muscular and her shoulders broad, like those of a swimmer, although she never swam.

The typical teenage "baby fat" showed up here and there, but even that made her more attractive to him. Jake smiled as he looked from her ankles to her eyes. He noticed her toenails were painted with little yellow daisies and that she wore a gold bracelet on her left ankle. Her feet were bare. He totally approved! His gaze stopped on her chest. This girl had breasts the size of cantaloupes and he couldn't wait to take one of them into his mouth!

"Jakey!" Sindra exclaimed, her breasts jiggled as she jumped with delight at seeing him. She flew into his arms. The smile she flashed him showed her excitement at his arrival.

Sindra hugged him tightly. She was truly glad to see him. Jake smiled. He drew her closer so he could feel those firm breasts against his chest. Oh God, how he wanted her, right here, right now! But there would be time for all that later. He savored the feel of a woman fully against his body, especially this one. Head to foot hugs were the very best feeling in the world, well, second only to the release that came with hot, mind blowing sex. And he loved how Sindra felt against his body, in his arms.

Jake didn't want to let go of her but drew back long enough to greet her then pulled her to him again.

"Hiya Cupcake. It is soooooooooo good to see you." He held her close and grinded his hips into her a bit. He noticed she didn't protest at all rather leaned into him and squeezed her arms tighter around his waist.

"Guess what, Jakey?" Sindra raised her head from his chest so she could see his face; her eyes were dancing with little monkey-shines.

"What?" Jake pulled back as well so he could focus on those incredible blue eyes.

"We have the apartment just to ourselves. I told everyone else this was MY time and they weren't going to screw it up." She hugged Jake again, pressing into him even harder. She knew exactly what she was doing to him. She could feel him grow and harden as she moved her hips into him.

"I see" said Jake, the sly grin on his face showed his amusement. "How 'bout if we go to dinner and come back and see what kind of trouble we can get into?" He grinned and pinched one of her breasts, erecting a nipple.

"I have a better idea, Jakey…let's skip dinner. If you are hungry later, I promise we can get something, but right now, all I want is you. We keep talking and talking about it. I want action!" She grabbed his shirt and dragged him into the living room slamming the front door behind them.

Jake kissed her with such savageness he knew her lips had to hurt, but he just simply didn't care. This seemed to be what she wanted. He tore at her clothes, tossing them here and there. He grabbed her hair and forced her to her knees in front of him. She gave him a devilish grin. Oh, yeah, he was going to enjoy this, maybe way too much.

He removed the rest of his clothes and stood naked before her….hands on his hips. She was still kneeling in front of him, staring at his erection, knowing what would be next.

Jake pushed her head toward his hardness. He grabbed her hair and pulled her to him so her mouth surrounded his shaft. Sindra did what she was being forced to do and did it willingly. She could barely breathe. This was such a turn on! The more he pulled on her hair, the more of a turn on it was. She moaned. He didn't know if it was in pain or in ecstasy, but he didn't care as long as she continued moving her mouth. She was driving him crazy. She seemed very well versed in what she was doing and it made Jake wonder just how many other men she had given blow jobs to.

She took her time, even though Jake's promptings were more savage and more intentional for her to be rough with him. She moved her mouth from his shaft to his inner thighs and began biting his skin sending incredible shock-like pulses into his hardness, making him want to fill her mouth all the more.

Jake couldn't tolerate this any longer, he needed to be inside her, needed to fill her with all of him she could handle.

He pulled her up to a standing position by her hair and pushed her over the couch so her tight ass faced him. He fingered her with one hand and with the other pinched and teased the taut nipple of her breast. He wanted to make sure she was wet, wanting him as he wanted her. Once he entered her he began pumping into her hard and fast, he heard her screams but he just kept going, his release was too close to stop now. Jake could tell by the feel of her that this was her first time, that he was the first person to completely take her.

It really surprised him because they had discussed sexual experiences in past conversations. Even though most of what they talked about seemed to involve hand or oral stimulation, Jake figured she was equally knowledgeable with the rest of it. He hadn't given any thought to the fact that there was never penetration until him, and that excited him all the more, making him move faster inside of her.

Amongst the screams and the tears he heard her plead, "Harder, Jakey, faster!" Sindra almost yelled the words at him. And he didn't need to be told twice. Oh God, she felt so warm and so alive! His hands were wrapped around her breasts and his fingers pinched her tender but hardened nipples. He loved how tight she felt around him and he could feel her clamping down on him as they climaxed together. Jake took his own sweet time to slow his movements and eventually collapsed, exhausted, on top of Sindra's back. He stayed there, still inside of her, still gently fondling her breasts until his breathing returned to somewhat normal then he moved off of her.

He stood there naked, looking at her as she stood up to face him, tears stained her cheeks. "Oh my God, Cupcake, come here," Jake sighed, and took her into his arms, placing a tender kiss on the top of her head. "Are you okay? Why didn't you tell me?" He asked as he brushed her hair from her face and gently wiped her tears with his thumbs. There was true concern in Jake's voice and that amazed even him.

"Jakey, don't worry about it. I'm fine…really. It was wonderful. You were wonderful." She smiled and pulled his head down to her level and kissed him. "Pain with you is ecstasy," she said, trying to reassure him, and her, as she still felt the ache from the harshness of their coming together. "I wanted to experience this, you, and I'm not sorry we did this at all. I am glad you were my first. I trust you." She released him and began picking up clothes and putting them on.

"I can't believe we did this." Jake said, running a hand through his sweaty hair. "Are you hungry?" he asked as he tucked in his shirt and buckled his belt. He already knew what the reply would be but figured he could go get something for her if she wanted.

Sindra shook her head. "No, I am not, but thank you. I have to get this stack of homework done yet tonight," she pointed to the books and papers that were now scattered all over the floor. "Semester ends next week and then I am done until fall. I have Ramen in the cupboard. I'll be fine." She assured him.

"Cupcake, I hate to leave you like this. I want to make sure you are okay. I didn't hurt you too badly, did I?" Jake asked, his hand on her cheek. Again his concern and tenderness toward Sindra surprised him. "I have to finish packing for this Japan trip. I wish I could whisk you away from all this, just take you with me." Jake tenderly smiled at her.

Sindra wrapped her arms around herself. "Jakey, it's okay. I told you, it's all good, so stop worrying. You didn't hurt me. You felt amazing inside me. Now go before you are late." She lightly smacked him on the arm.

Jake kissed the top of her head, then dipped his head down and kissed her lips, tenderly, sweetly, not like the first kiss. He made his way to the door. "I'm not sure when I'll be back from Japan, but I'll check in on you, ok? Take care, Cupcake." He bent down and hugged her tightly again and left another tender kiss on her lips.

Sindra held him a bit longer before letting him go.

"Travel safe, Jakey. I'll miss you." A tear ran down her cheek.

"No tears Cupcake, okay? I will be back. We'll be together again soon, I promise. After today there's no way I will stay away from you now."

Jake walked to the door and put his hand on the doorknob but couldn't open the door. He turned to Sindra and took her in his arms again, squeezing her tight then dropped another kiss the top of her head.

"I'll call you the instant I get back into town. Get your homework done, eat something and relax, okay?"

Sindra nodded at him. Those damn blue eyes! He was going to be dreaming of them and this day for weeks to come. He walked through the door quietly pulling it shut behind him and made his way down the walk to his car.

He really, truly cared for this young girl. Ha! He really, truly cared for each of the women with whom he had sex. And then there was that thought again, creeping out of the box he thought he had locked and shoved to the back corner of his brain.

Regardless of how beautiful women were, regardless of how old or young they were, regardless of how experienced or inexperienced they were sexually, regardless of their financial or social status, not one compared to Jillian on any level. Yet, he still needed the feeling from the adrenaline rush of the hunt and kill when there were new prospects. He needed to feel the diversity of female bodies. There was something so satisfying, so self-gratifying in knowing he could please them all. He smiled.

He opened the door to his vehicle and climbed in. Jake began coughing, and coughing so hard he brought up blood. This wasn't the first time that had happened. He took a drink from the water bottle that was in the cup holder. It had been sitting there in the sun the past few hours and scalded his mouth and throat, but helped quell the cough. He reached in the "trinket" holder, which really was the ashtray, and grabbed a couple antacids and popped them in his mouth.

He checked his hair in the rearview mirror and saw Sindra standing in the doorway smiling at him. Jake returned her smile with one of his own and waved out the open top of the car. He cranked the radio and pulled away from the curb.

Queen's "Another One Bites the Dust" sounded from the radio and Jake let out a hearty laugh. How appropriate!

CHAPTER TEN

Sultry Sensations opened with grand reviews and the neighboring stores welcomed her to "their" street. That in itself was something and a bit of a surprise, considering. It was the first time that a shop such as hers, an upscale lingerie and adult toy shop for women, was allowed to be a business in the city of Acorn Hills, let alone be on this block in the newly renovated portion of town. After much discussion at town meetings and with her promise to do tasteful window displays, the other business owners agreed that Sultry Sensations could be a drawing card for them as well.

Even then it took Denise Berrie several months and several meetings debating over whether it was "appropriate" to sell such things and to market the idea that women were sensual, warm human beings with needs and desires. It seemed that the good ole' boy mentality that had once run the Council of this city was dwindling, and because of that and the young members with fresh ideas, she got her foot in the door…and by God she was not moving now that she was established!

Denise had a knack of doing very bright, very eye catching window displays and because the shops were so close together in this new district, it was easy to allow your eyes to travel from one window to the one next to it, even though it was a different business. The particular variety of shops was a true drawing card to this part of Acorn Hills. You really wouldn't have to go to the outlying areas to shop unless you needed to go to a Shop-All or lower end clothing store or something along those lines. The square offered all you could want from locally owned shops.

Yes indeed, from the Fortune 500 consulting firm, Evans Enterprises, to a world renowned antique dealer, a pastry/catering shop, floral shop and Turners Bar and Grill, and several other clothing and trinket stores; you could purchase what you wanted, take your time doing it, go have a drink and eat something and best of all support the local business owners.

Denise was flattered by the words the townspeople had uttered at the meetings about her choice to be in this location as well as for the need for her products. She was very thankful for the new people who seemed to continually bring fresh ideas to the Chamber meetings and weren't afraid to speak up and support them.

When this was only a slim glimmer of an idea, Denise asked friends to host several "in home" shows of her products, offering door prizes and other incentives if others booked parties. So, when Sultry Sensations opened, much of the town was ready and primed for a shop like hers, and it had done banner sales from day one. When the Governor's wife phoned to say she was planning a "party", actually a fundraiser, and wanted several lingerie items for her guests, Denise jumped at the chance to fill the order.

She had no idea at that time that the volume she would have to order was more than her normal in-store stock for the semi-annual sale she had hopes of planning. After carefully pouring over the lingerie catalogues, Mrs. Sutter had ordered 300 different lingerie items, the majority of them being imports.

Countless phone calls to irate Italian designers and fabric mills yielded nothing. Denise still couldn't tell Mrs. Sutter when the lingerie would arrive, nor could she assure the woman the items would get there in time for the fundraiser. It was very embarrassing for Denise to be in this predicament, especially when this could either make or break her business. And it was especially aggravating knowing it was out of her hands!

She put her pen down and answered the phone.

"Sultry Sensations, this is Denise."

When you heard her, she was simply sensual! There was no other way of describing it. There was this deep richness to her voice and it was though she cast a spell on those she spoke with, no one could turn down her sales pitch. She sounded like what liquid dark chocolate tasted: sweet, warm, inviting, and too damn sexy for her own good!

"Hi, Darlin'. How ya doin?" was the chipper reply on the other end of the phone.

"David!" Denise breathed a sigh of relief. "You have no idea how glad I am to hear you! I've just had a ghastly morning. I'm worried about Jillian and then on top of that, the shipment of imported Italian lingerie I've been waiting for, the one for the Governor's wife's party? Well, it's been back ordered, yet again! Oh, David, I don't know what to do! This is the largest, single most important order I have received since opening. It was going to bring in the revenue I was so counting on for the rest of the season." Denise was close to tears.

"Honey, please calm down. You aren't doing anyone any good getting all worked up like that. If you want, I can come over and see what I can do before I go to the bar." He offered. Although he wasn't sure exactly what he could do, other than be there for moral support. He knew nothing about the things she sold at Sultry Sensations, nor did he want to, unless of course she was wearing one of them.

"And, I know what you mean about Jillian. She wasn't in too good of shape when I last saw her. But, you know she IS going to be okay. She's handled far worse things than this." David tried reassuring Denise, but he knew his words were falling on deaf ears.

"Thank you for the offer of coming over to help. But, honey, I don't want to make you crazy, too. One of us in that state is more than enough at this point." Even in her attempt to be funny her weariness was very noticeable even over the phone.

"Babe, I'm just so tired of getting the run around. I was assured these items would be here last week. Then, last week, I was assured delivery today. Now they're "going to get back to me." My last effort is to put a tracking on it. If I hear 'but signore' one more time, I WILL pull that flipping little Italian snob through the phone!"

Denise's voice became louder and louder the longer she spoke.

"I can't stand this!" She was crying now. "I want my business to succeed and I want Mrs. Sutter to be happy; and a happy Governor's wife, means, hopefully, a booming business for me because of the referrals. And yet, here I sit waiting on empty promises from people who are making me look bad.

"Oh, David, what the hell am I doing? Maybe I just shouldn't have even thought I could do something like this." She put her head in her free hand and still clutched her cell phone to her ear with the other.

Denise could hear David trying to calm her down, but she couldn't distinguish the words because she was sobbing so hard.

She loved this man so much. They had known each other for a while now. It was an instant over-the-moon type thing when they met. There wasn't anything that one wouldn't do for the other. It was as though they were the second skin of each other. And, to look at them, you'd never have put them together.

David was a Vietnam vet and an old hippie; quiet, proper, always thinking, always busy-with-a-project type of guy and she was from the wrong side of the tracks. She grew up on welfare and had to wear hand-me-downs most of her life. But as it so often does, somehow the Fates seemed to know they needed each other and so they were together, and very happily together.

Secretly Denise was hoping it was a forever kind of together, but she couldn't let her mind wander down that rabbit hole right now. She needed to get to the bottom of why her order was not there and what the hell she would have to do to get it filled on time. If she had to fly to Italy and bring back the lingerie, she would do it! That is how desperate she had become.

There was going to be so much to do when that order arrived. The lingerie needed to be dry-cleaned, pressed and she needed to find models with figures that would highlight the uniqueness of each piece. She and Mrs. Sutter would just have to sit down and go over the invitation list for the models.

Denise wanted to make sure she made her money on this project, but more so she wanted to make sure the items brought top dollar for the auction and fund raiser. She knew how close this event was to Mrs. Sutter's heart. She wanted it, no, NEEDED it to be perfect!

"Alright, honey, I understand. And I know without a shadow of doubt that you can handle any "signor" with your wit and grace but if you need me, all ya gotta do is call, okay? I'm off to work. I have a shipment of booze to check in. How 'bout you join me there for dinner, say around sixish?" David laughed again, trying to lighten her mood. "Hell, I'll even buy!"

Denise laughed and rolled her eyes. "Great, bar food, yet again." She replied, the dimples in her cheeks showing with her broad smile. "I'm teasing, honey. The only perk of having dinner at the bar is that I get to spend time with my one and only. You mean the world to me. Thanks for wanting to help. I love you, David."

"So, I'll see you later?" David prompted, really hoping she would take enough time to eat, but more so to just get away from this project that was driving her bonkers.

"Yes, dear man, I'll be there for onion rings and a couple lime-a-ritas around six. I think I'll see if Jillian wants to join us," she made a kissing noise into the phone receiver. "Ciao."

"Ciao, Bella."

Denise re-cradled her cell phone on its charger and looked at the invoice staring back at her. There HAD to be a reason why this order wasn't here and she was going to track it down come hell or high water! No way was she going to disappoint Mrs. Sutter or the hundreds of other women who would be getting their first glimpse of what Sultry Sensations offered.

Denise took pride in the fact that her shop was so much more than an "intimate" clothing store or an adult "toy" shop for women. It was a coming of age place where friends brought friends; where women met new friends; where new experiences were discussed and future experiences were planned. It was where questions could be asked in a safe environment and where no one would belittle you for your lack of knowledge or your prowess of too much knowledge. Denise wanted to make sure that all women had the chance to explore their sexuality that is why Sultry Sensations was born.

Her shop had the potential of being a haven for those who were naïve as well as those with the most sexual experience…women learning from other women. Women needed to feel secure about who they were, how special they were, how much being a sensual, sexual person meant. She wanted to do the best and be the best at her trade and she was going to do just that.

    Denise had struggled most of her life. If it wasn't one thing it was another. Her life had been a dramatic roller coaster ride from high school until she decided one day that she was worthy enough of self-appreciation. That was when she turned the corner, met David and began this adventure.

    It was so important to her to make a difference in the lives of those around her. Society deserved people who were truly educated about life and all it held; and a part of that was knowledge of your own body and emotions. Denise's passion was that women, all women of any age, should have the freedom to know who they are and know to react to the sensations of their own bodies. If that could happen maybe teenage pregnancies and STD's would decrease.

    That was one of the reasons why she didn't hesitate when Mrs. Sutter asked her for her help for the fundraiser. All Denise could see was the opportunity to touch a lot of women at the same time. And right now, she had to make sure that was a happening thing.

    Okay, now, where was that phone number? Denise scanned the invoice in her hand and spotted the phone number in the upper right hand corner. She grabbed the portable business phone; punching numbers with gusto. A male voice speaking very quickly, in Italian, of course answered the phone.

    " Ciao come può l'aiuto." Did all Italian men have the power to want you to jump them just by hearing their voices? She smiled. Shame on me for those thoughts.

    Denise replied. "Hello, yes you may help me. I'd like to speak with the owner of your shop, please."

    She was promptly put on hold with the customary "elevator music" only in a foreign language. Four songs later someone finally spoke.

    "Yes" the male voice said.

    "Signor, this is Denise Berrie, owner of Sultry Sensations, in America and we need to talk. You have 300 pieces of my product and I want to know where the hell they are and when I can expect them to arrive at my business!"

CHAPTER ELEVEN

The sweet, heady floral fragrance that hit you as you walked through the door of Special Occasions was like none other. Your eye was immediately drawn to the brightly lit display cooler. Shelves held pre-made arrangements and on the floor were buckets of flowers…yellow, orange, pink and red Asiatic lilies; lavender, grape, peach, cream and white spikes of stock; Stargazer lilies in the traditional fuchsia/pink/burgundy and the massive fully open white Casa Blanca. One section of the cooler was designated to roses—several shades of red, yellow, white, pink and lavender as well as smaller buckets of sweetheart spray roses in all colors. Another section was devoted to the "standards" in floral arranging; carnations in every color, as well as daisies, cushion mums, Fuji mums and assorted fillers and greenery including baby's breath, wax flower, Italian ruscus, myrtle and variegated boxwood.

Antique windows decorated with various silk ivy and floral garlands hung on the walls of the show room. Several glass and brass stands sported silk arrangements. A round three tier gray stone fountain in the front window set up the perfect place for the plants to reside. The floor was a faux brick vinyl which was very easy to clean, one of the reasons Jillian chose that particular style when she put this building together. Concrete benches and memory stones on easels were placed among the plants and here and there tucked into shelves were stuffed animals and stone angels and other trinkets that she felt appropriate to sell that could also be used as "add-ons" to her floral designs.

Opposite the front counter was an old but well taken care of round oak table with wire service books and wedding and sympathy books from which customers could browse and choose floral arrangements.

The front counter was organized but cluttered with the customary enclosure cards on spin racks and matching envelopes and the computer/cash register/floral receiving order system. A brightly colored plastic box held pens for her customers to sign cards.

Behind that counter was a small sink and work space with every tool you could imagine, every gauge wire, floral tape, and any other supplies that would be needed to process the product or to create beautiful arrangements for the clients who walked through the door. This was Jillian's work space. An old backless barstool covered in black leather sat between the counters.

Above her work center was a huge open window so she could see into the main design room and grab product or for her workers to acknowledge customers when they came in. It made things a lot more efficient to be able to use the space from both sides.

On the other side of the pass through window was where the "real" work happened. The dried product and most of the silks were housed back there and the cooler was accessible as well, where the surplus fresh product was stored. Several work stations were fully set up. This was where her employees hung out and created new wreaths and bouquets and beautiful designs that amazed her on a daily basis.

In this spacious work area, floor to ceiling steel shelving units held every kind of container imaginable: glass cubes, bud vases, colored vases, low centerpiece containers, novelty birthday, new baby, sympathy, baskets, and even a few special pieces for (so far) one-time events like young Maria's Quinceanera and Benjamin's Bar Mitzvah.

Three wooden and glass enclosed cases held ribbons of every color in every fabric…tulle, double edged satin, wired, unwired, picot in sizes from 1/8" to 5" wide. Two six foot long tables were placed next to the ribbon cupboards. This is where the completed orders for delivery were checked one last time before Alex took them to the van that was parked in the adjacent heated/cooled garage.

As you continued to the back of the store from the display cooler, a locked wrought iron privacy gate was decorated with ecru lace curtains to soften the look and make it fit in more with the rest of the interior's aesthetics. It led to the upstairs of the building. Upstairs was a wonderful 3 bedroom one and a half bath apartment complete with fireplace and hardwood floors. Her dream was to finish the apartment so she could sell her parents' home and move into it at some point. She kept telling herself "someday." But so far, someday hadn't happened. For the time being renting a condo not far from the shop seemed like the thing to do. It had adequate space for her as well as for Jake's things. Okay we are NOT going to go down that road right now. I have way too much to do. She scolded herself.

Jillian had arrived at the shop early hoping to get a start on processing the flowers for the wedding on Saturday. It was already Thursday and she wanted to make absolutely sure the flowers would be open when she began working on the bouquets Friday, then fully open on Saturday so their beauty could be appreciated. As she turned the key and opened the door to the shop, again she thought "I MUST get that upstairs apartment finished." She entered the shop and re-locked the door. She still had two hours before she was officially open and while she usually didn't mind early hour walk-ins this time she truly needed that time to get things organized for the big weekend!

The table was mounded with ribbons and a stack of wedding books. They usually were housed in the bookshelf just to the left of the table, but someone must have come in last night for a consultation. Jillian had enough faith in her employees that she told them if they could generate the business, they could do the full consultation themselves and get a commission on what was sold. They all worked hard to please her. They all, Jillian included, loved Special Occasions and the recognition that it was gaining traction with the community and beyond as word continued to spread regarding the quality of her product and service.

Jillian picked up the books and put them in their rightful place, grabbed a paper towel and sprayed disinfectant and wiped down the table, pushing the chairs in so as not to trip over them. She wiped down the front counter as well.

She made her way to the sink and squirted floral preservative in the container she was running water in and lifted it to the counter. She grabbed six blocks of Oasis foam, floated them in the container and watched them as they sank and absorbed the water. They would be ready for arrangements as soon as her team arrived. She grabbed her knife and cut the rope holding the 5 boxes together that were stacked by the sink. The older she got the more she appreciated the fact that there were stands and she didn't have to bend and lift things too far.

Jillian removed the lid from box number one and carefully surveyed the contents. Giant white calla lilies who's heads were shielded and stamens wrapped with cotton greeted her as did several bunches of pristine white roses, three boxes of stephanotis, two bunches of white wax flower and a bunch of variegated mini-pittosporum. She smiled. If all the boxes she opened looked like this the wedding would turn out beautiful! Fabulous! Her mind wandered as she began cutting the stems under water then placing the flowers in buckets of warm water with floral preservative solution.

The only thing holding her back about the apartment upstairs was selling from the house her parents' gave her back when they moved to the senior living center on the edge of town fifteen years ago. The house was still filled with memories of growing up…not to mention literally filled with everything that a fifty nine year marriage collected!

She needed to call her brother, Chris, and have him block out a space of time when the two of them could just go through everything, take what was theirs, and make decisions on selling the rest.

Sylvia, Jillian's mother, had been the first to go. She became very ill with pneumonia and her frail body couldn't fight off the infections. It wasn't long after that her dad, Bob, passed as well. Chris and Mary lived four hours away and seldom returned to Acorn Hills, so she had been left with the details of two funerals as well as the will reading and what to do with the items in the house as well as THE house.

She would be the first to admit she was in denial of her parents' deaths. Maybe that was why she just couldn't live in that house, too many memories. It seemed like only yesterday when her mom and dad would walk into the shop on 4th Street. It was her father who encouraged her to move into her current building when this new district was renovated following the flood.

"Jillian", he had said "you can't go wrong. It's the up and coming place around here and I know you'll just knock it outta the park if you move. Where you are now is in an area with all of us old people. Soon there won't be any old people left; you need some young blood in the store. You need to think about that, darlin' girl."

For as long as she could remember her parents had their offices in their home so they could be available for their children. Even when they had the opportunity to move into a building, together they opted to still do business from their home. She was very hesitant to leave the 4th street shop, but after her dad told her to move, she figured, what the heck. So, she moved and it didn't take long to figure out it was the right decision!

Opening day was incredible at this location! Her father had been right. She remembered her parents coming into the shop and looking around and her father hugging her with tears in his eyes, whispering in her ear "you'll be just fine, darlin' girl, just fine. I'm so proud of you!"

Jillian wiped a tear that had found its way down her cheek. She loved her dad so much and there was such a great loss in her soul when he died. She didn't think she could ever get over the pain of losing him. She and her Mom were close, sure, but nothing would ever take the place of those early morning walks with Dad, or the late night phone calls when she was in college when she wondered if a business degree was really what she wanted to go for. He always encouraged her to follow her heart. So, she finished the business degree, but she also began dabbling a bit in the floral industry. She found she had a true eye for color, line and design so she took a few night courses "just for fun".

Time passes at race horse speed the older you get. How many times had she heard that in her youth? The past fifteen years had just flown by. Jillian's dream was to be able to work for a company that would fully appreciate what she had to offer. Her marketing skills were top notch and she could write proposals like none other. However, after not really finding what she wanted in the job market, she opened Special Occasions.

There was so much she wanted to do with her shop. She was already ranked by the locals as one of the best floral shops in Acorn Hills, and the growing reputation even among surrounding towns showed the attention was growing. But she wanted to really be on the cutting edge with the newest designs and the newest products. She wanted to be different and she wanted people to know that her work was the absolute best quality you could find anywhere and that she stood behind everything that went out her door.

Originally Jillian had one helper when she had The Shop on 4th, and since moving had to hire two other designers and her older son, Alex, as the full time delivery person. Jillian still designed, still kept her hand on quality control of flowers and products, still did most of the wedding bouquets and casket sprays for funerals and of course still did her own books (after all, that WAS what her degree was for). Being in your mid-fifties didn't afford you much time to achieve the dreams of your youth when you didn't get started until well after you were forty!

She finished processing the new flowers, checked all of the plants to make sure they were not wilted and watered those that were, heaved a sigh and started for the door to put the "open" sign up, when her cell phone rang.

"Morning, Mom." It was Alex.

"Hi honey. Are you okay? What's up?" Jillian sounded concerned.

"Yes and nothing. I just wondered if you wanted me to bring coffee and breakfast when I come in this morning. I didn't know if you had had time to grab anything before you left home or not and I worry about you, Mom."

Alex was the more level headed of her two boys. He had followed his mother's steps and gone to college and got his business degree as well. After sending out resume after resume and hearing nothing in the job market, he jumped at the chance to work with his mom when she offered the delivery job to him. He realized it wasn't making what he would if he was with a bigger company, but it did give him the money to pay for his own place and also allowed him to keep an eye on his mom and help as he could.

Alex decided he needed to take the reins of responsibility since his younger brother was off playing music with some band somewhere. He stayed behind and felt it was his duty to make sure his mom was okay. Devon just seemed to march to his own drummer. He always had, so after school, he took off to see the world and experience all he could experience. He checked in occasionally, but not as often as Alex would like him to, and certainly not as often as Jillian wanted. Besides being in Acorn Hills right now would allow Alex to hopefully have another chance with his high school sweetheart, Felicia, who had moved back to Acorn Hills. She had accepted the position of Dean of Coral Knoll Community College.

"Oh, Alex, coffee would be wonderful!" Jillian replied.

"White chocolate mocha decaf with whip?" she could hear the amusement in her son's voice as he stated exactly the same thing at the same time and both laughed at what had happened.

"Yes, please. See ya when ya get here. And Alex? Thanks!"

"Yeah, yeah, no problem, Mom."

She closed her phone, tucked it safely back in the pocket of her jeans and looked at the clock. Fifteen minutes until it was business as usual. Even though it was early she unlocked the door anyway and put the "open" sign up, walked back to the front counter and grabbed a pen. She found a piece of paper and at the top wrote THINGS I NEED (the word underlined several times) TO GET DONE. The first item she listed was "apartment".

CHAPTER TWELVE

There was absolutely nothing better at 6 a.m. than the smell of freshly brewing coffee. Richard closed his eyes and raised his arms high above his head and stretched until he could see little spots behind his eye lids, exploding in anticipation of another morning. He took a deep breath of the blessed aroma-it smelled like a new day! His bare feet patted to the refrigerator freezer and he took out a couple frozen cinnamon rolls from Ginger's bakery, put them on a plate and in the microwave to thaw and warm. He grabbed the butter and coffee creamer from the refrigerator as well, setting them on the table as he walked by and gently kicked the refrigerator door shut with his left heel.

    Richard stretched again, only this time bending to the floor. He thought how good it felt as he reached even lower hearing the vertebrae and tight muscles of his back crackle. Getting older just sucked! He stood up and ran a hand over his military-cut hair or at least what was left of it. He certainly was not a young man any more, but there was no way he would trade his life and how it had been lived for another shot. Why change anything when it led him to a place where he was so happy with who he was and what he had been through?

    He loved school, loved sports, enjoyed his friends, even enjoyed serving his country in Viet Nam, and now truly had found what he had been seeking to fulfill the job aspect of his life. The only thing that was missing was that special lady who would make everything complete. Granted, he didn't need someone to complete HIM. He was a self-made man, strong, independent, and happy with his own company…as it should be.

But even though he did believe that, he would be the first to admit there was something missing…he did miss the touch of a woman in the décor of his home, in his business, but most of all in his personal life, in his heart. He wanted to spend the rest of his life with someone. He was tired of being an army of one. He wanted someone to wake up with, someone to share his hopes and dreams, someone to hold and comfort when THEY needed it, but secretly he needed someone to do that for him as well. He was lonely. He longed for what Denise and David had, what Ginger and Jordan had, hell as weird and degrading as it was even bits of what Jillian had with Jake. But just bits of that one.

He just could not figure out that relationship. A year into it he stopped trying. Jake was a smooth talker, a snake who would tell anyone anything at any point in time to get what he wanted. He was so not the type of guy Jillian usually ran with. Her husband, Brett, was a pain in the ass in high school, but overall he was a nice guy who really respected Jillian for the unique and wonderful woman she was and he loved his boys. But Jake, well, Jake was a different story.

Sure, in high school, Richard dated all of the cheerleaders at one time or another, but never at the same time. During his service time, there had been a couple of native women who had caught his fancy for a few months, a couple of the nurses who temporarily took his mind off where he was. He had always been charismatic, fun, and fairly good looking…and fearless. It helped pass the time in that hell hole, anyway, for him and for them, so why not?

And then he returned to Acorn Hills and saw Jillian, saw who she was involved with and also saw how unhappy she really was with Jake. Richard and Jillian were best friends growing up and they remained that way until he left for Viet Nam. He remembered being at the airport and giving her a hug and in a rare moment of openness saying "Jilly, just remember you're my best friend ever and if I don't come back" and at that moment Jillian put her finger to his lips to stop the next words and just gave him this all-encompassing hug that seemed to last forever. He remembered that as he boarded the plane to leave, Jillian waved and wiped a tear away.

Was it so silly of him to think that even now there could be something between them? Something more than the friendship they had nurtured all these years? Or was that all just false hope? Was it all just a fantasy, a dream that haunted his very soul?

Richard poured coffee into the mug that already held the creamer and took the cinnamon rolls from the microwave before sitting down at the kitchen table. He knew that Jillian had a lot she was dealing with emotionally…the loss of both parents in a year's time, a younger son who couldn't seem to be respectful to his mother, and now the break-up of what seemed to be the ideal relationship. Not to mention the loss of her husband, Brett. He knew that she still hadn't fully dealt with the accident or his death.

Saying he was concerned about her was an understatement. All he could do is be as available to her as she would allow. She looked tired all the time, pale almost. He didn't want to seem pushy with all this. Maybe he should suggest taking the boat out on the lake this weekend; call Ginger and Jordan and David and Denise and just make a party of it. He made a mental note to do just that after he got to the store.

The walnut grandfather clock in the living room chimed seven times. Richard sighed audibly. How could an hour have already passed? He cherished the early morning quiet when he could sit and think, have his coffee and breakfast sweet and center himself for the day. It was a routine he established once he got home from the war. It gave him peace, sort of. He was tired this morning. A new shipment of antique oak furniture arrived yesterday and unloading it was a pain! The pieces were large, bulky, and weighed a ton. The muscles in his torso and upper legs could attest to that! On days like this his body told him how old he actually was!

But he was sure his customers would find it very beautiful and hopefully purchase it all. He rose from the table, tossed the paper plate in the trash and ran water in the coffee cup, leaving it in the sink, and made his way to ready for the day.

He placed his hands on the light gray tile shower wall in front of him. As the hot water pelted the nape of his neck and ran down his back, he couldn't stop thinking of Jillian and about how upset she was the day that she told Jake to get his things, how she tried to cover up her feelings by drinking herself into a stupor. It just was so not her. He had never known her to reach for the bottle for consolation. Ice cream, yes; booze, no.

Stopping at the store on his way home for ice cream had been the right thing to do. Just as he thought, she did call the following day for "ice cream therapy" and they sat on her couch in silence for the longest time. Richard finally just grabbed the spoon from her and reached out to her and held her as she sobbed into his shoulder.

When she gained composure, she explained to Richard exactly what had been happening the past few years and why she was so distraught. He tried reassuring her that it was all going to be as it should be. She had Ginger and Denise, and him, of course, to help in whatever way they all could to make it easier for her to accept the fact that Jake the Snake was indeed just that, a snake. He remembered how angry he was because someone had hurt her so deeply and how much she was anguishing over all of it.

Stepping out of the shower and drying the water beads from his body, his thoughts continued. What if, finally, there could be something between him and Jillian? What if for the first time she really knew exactly how he felt about her? He shook his head and muttered to himself…like that will happen! But the other part of him said, make it happen! What have you got to lose?

Richard pulled a pair of jeans from the drawer of the antique pine dresser and went to the closet for a black tee shirt with the Richard's Relics embroidered logo on the left side pocket. He tucked in his shirt, fastened his belt and secured his cell phone holder through one of the loops. He ran a brush through his short hair out of military precision habit, grabbed another bottle and splashed on something that smelled good, latched his watch around his wrist, picked up his Doc Martins and headed toward the living room.

He glanced at the clock again as it chimed 8:15 a.m. Instead of waiting until he got to work he could make the phone calls before he left. It was late enough to begin calling people, he hoped. Sitting down on the sofa, he picked up the cordless phone and began punching numbers.

"Hello?" the voice on the other end sounded awake with eyes wide open and Richard felt relieved.

"David? It's Richard. Hey, I have a plan for part of the weekend, was wondering if you and Denise could get away. I thought we would take the boat out to the lake Sunday and just laze around all day, picnic and such. I plan to call Ginger too and see if she and Jordan would come along…as well as Jillian", Richard added, as he pulled on first one sock then the other, still cradling the phone between his ear and shoulder.

"Hey, Richard! That sounds wonderful. I'll have to run it past Denise, of course, but I know I need a break and I'm sure she would welcome one after dealing with all the Italian assholes she has had to deal with this week. Put us down as a yes, but I will call you tomorrow for sure to confirm." David paused for a moment before continuing. "I think Jillian needs this, too. Denise and I have been very concerned about her after the Jake incident. She just isn't the same. Like she is just going through the motions, ya know?" There was true concern in David's voice.

"Yeah, I know. That's why I am doing this, really. She does need to get away and she does need to be with people who care about her and she needs to forget that bastard. He better never come across my path because I can't guarantee that I won't deck the son-of-a-bitch!"

David laughed. "I'll hold him for you!"

Richard laughed as well "Hey, I'm going to try to get a hold of Ginger now before I leave for the store. Keep in touch, David."

And with that Richard pushed the off button. He slid his foot into one of the shoes then the other. He tried to not put them on until the very last minute. He hated shoes! It probably came from the foot rot from the boots he had to wear in Nam. Some habits are ingrained for such good reason they're just not going anywhere, no matter how many years go by in the meantime.

Richard tried Ginger's number next and Jordan answered the phone. He explained to Jordan the plan and Jordan was all for it saying that Ginger really needed the break too before the next catering jobs she had lined up because there were several large ones in a row.

Richard and Jordan continued visiting a while longer then Richard ended the conversation with a "see ya Sunday" and hung up the phone. He grabbed the keys to his black Nitro and headed out the door. He sighed. Now, all he needed to do was convince Ms. Jilly that this was in HER best interest as well.

There was still time to do just that before he had to open his shop at 10. A taste of her own medicine may just do the trick, he thought raising an eyebrow and grinning at the brilliant idea. Yes, coffee and something sweet from the bakery just may do it. So he set out to get those things from Ginger's shop and take them next door to the flower lady who had so many years ago unexpectedly stolen his heart and never given it back.

CHAPTER THIRTEEN

The streets were full of people carrying packages, a normal sight in Tokyo. The heavy smell of onion and garlic and teriyaki filled the air. Even though it was a modern city, Tokyo still embraced a lot of the old ways.

It was such an eclectic city…while some were dressed in very traditional clothing, some in suits and ties, most of those over 60 yrs. of age walked with satchels that held their purchases.

Expressways crisscrossed the city of Tokyo and Narita International airport was one of the finest in the world. It was in the small villages where modern met traditional. The side streets in small villages were home to open air markets that sold everything from seafood to fruit to trinkets of every shape and size. It was a very busy, very noisy city.

Hearing sirens was normal fare in large cities such as Tokyo. The sound of screaming ambulance sirens cut through the afternoon buzz on the busy street in Japan. Whatever was going on was a "STAT call" because the vehicle traveled at breakneck speed as it screeched up to the emergency doors of the hospital. Onlookers saw a body on a stretcher being wheeled very quickly through the ER doors as several ambulance attendants administered CPR and checked various tubes.

"Move! Get out of my way! Bring him into room three!" People were shouting over one another, getting necessary attention in an attempt to accomplish what each needed to get done.

Nurses were hooking up monitors, inserting ports for IV's, taking blood pressure, putting oxygen over the patient's nose and mouth and recording all the data they could get. Several doctors were barking orders to do this test and that test and get the results back as soon as possible. The man on the stretcher lay there, lifeless, barely breathing. There were no apparent external injuries. This puzzled the doctors. "He's lost a lot of blood," said one of the EMT's. "What did you say happened and where?" The attending physician quizzed one of the ambulance attendants.

"All we know is there was a call for us to go to Narita International Airport. That is where we found him on the moving sidewalk. He was in bad shape then."

Monitors began beeping warnings to the ER staff. Blood pressure numbers were not good. It appeared he wasn't going to survive.

"Damn it, don't you dare die on my watch." The attending physician demanded of the lifeless form on the table as the medical staff continued working to save his life.

The cardiac monitor sounded a continuous beep signaling a flat-line.

"CODE BLUE, CODE BLUE, GET THE CRASH CART STAT!" Gelling the paddles and placing them on his chest the doctor yelled "CLEAR" and everyone moved back.

Once, twice no response. Third time, no response.

"Goddamn it." the doctor took of his gloves and looked at the clock. "Call it." He directed his words to the paramedic to his left.

"Time of death 6:02 p.m." The paramedic stated, pulled off his gloves and hung his head.

The attending physician requested the hospital contact the Chief Medical Examiner to do an autopsy. It was always so difficult to lose a patient, especially when you really didn't have a clue why they were brought into the ER until the test results were completed. There was evidently something major that had happened to cause such bleeding, to cause his death.

****

This was the 4th flight in 4 months that Jake had taken to Tokyo to seal this Tomeiki deal. He had worked himself feverishly to near exhaustion trying to tie up these loose ends, so far to no avail. Today had to be the day. This was the final presentation. He had dotted every "I" and crossed every "T" a hundred times and he was tired of the monthly flights to and from Japan. Jake didn't let this get him down, though he had a feeling that this was going to go his way for a change.

Jake endured a simply miserable flight to Japan. He knew he was running a temperature and the cough kept getting worse. The last time he was in the airplane lavatory he was coughing up blood, and this wasn't just a few specks mixed in with the saliva. This time there was a lot of it.

He made his way back to his seat just as he heard the pilot announce they were to prepare for landing at Narita International Airport, the Tokyo airport that handled all of the international flights. He sat down and buckled up, leaning back to rest his head on the chair back. One of the gorgeous flight attendants looked at him and asked if he was okay and Jake just nodded, in too much pain to take advantage of an opportunity to flirt.

On a normal day, he would try everything in his power to flirt with them and maybe make plans for later for dinner and other things, but at this point nothing seemed to matter. He felt like shit. He had to impress a room full of people that he really wanted to purchase their corporation and add them to the ever growing holdings of Evans Enterprises, putting forward American confidence while also respecting the long list of behaviors for Japanese business culture.

He had to convince them that it was in THEIR best interest for their company as well as his and for the international market if they pooled their resources. The pain in his stomach was unbearable and the thought of "playing nice" made him just want to throw up. Truly all he wanted was to go home to Jillian, yet that would never happen again. He still thought of her even though they'd been a part for a while now. Jillian could always fix it, she could always make things better.

As passengers disembarked, Jake sat, got his bearings and let everyone else exit the plane. He slowly rose and grabbed his coat and luggage from the overhead compartment and made his way down the aisle of the plane and then into the airport to the right baggage claim and hopefully his ride to the hotel. The flight attendant asked if he was okay, touched his arm and bid him a good trip.

Jake smiled. Someone from Tomeiki was to meet him at the airport and take him to the hotel for a few hours of rest before the important meeting. He had looked at the presentation several times on the trip there. He knew that he didn't even need the portfolio he had with him, but it was papers with statistics they all could look at and keep. He had done this so many times that it was something he could do with his eyes shut. Now, if he could only get through it without another coughing attack, it would be miraculous! He reached baggage claim and saw his other suitcase on the turnaround and grabbed it when it came past. Not wasting any time he made his way through the throng of people outside to where he was told a car would be. There was a driver holding up a sign that said "Evans" and after spotting that, he walked over and greeted the man and got inside the limo.

It was a smooth ride to the hotel, and thank you travel gods, a short one, too! The hotel that Joni had booked was a five star hotel that was only a few blocks from the airport. The limo pulled up and the driver retrieved his bags and Jake put a twenty dollar bill in his hand and made his way into the hotel. He checked in at the front desk, was given instructions that his room was on the tenth floor and went to the elevator.

Once inside his room, Jake started shedding clothing the minute he hit the door and headed to the bathroom. The steam from the shower seemed to loosen the tightness in his chest and suddenly breathing wasn't so difficult. Maybe it was a virus or maybe it was just a chest cold. He'd had those before. But that didn't explain the stomach pain or the bleeding. Maybe it was the ulcer acting up again. God knows his life was the epitome of stress, and that was just when business was going well, not even with these constant visits to Tokyo and the personal issues he didn't want to think about.

This was just as well Jake knew he certainly didn't have time to worry about it now. In three hours he was to make this presentation before the Board of Directors of Tomeiki, Ltd. for the purchase of their business. He was to be infallible in his pitch, telling them how much Evans Enterprises needed a voice here in Japan and this was the way to do it. He turned the water off and grabbed a towel, dried off then wrapped it around his waist, walked back to the bed and fell back on it, staring at the ceiling falling victim to his mind wandering yet again.

"Damn you, Jillian!" he thought. "Damn you!" Thoughts of her plagued his dreams, his spare minutes…she infiltrated his life, his heart.

He missed her so much. He missed the way she felt in his arms. He missed her laugh. He missed the way she unconditionally loved him, no matter what. No matter how hard he tried, he couldn't forget her, couldn't stop thinking about her. He missed her! He set the alarm on his cell phone for an hour from now and covered up with the bedspread to help bring the sudden bout of shivering under control. He was freezing! Maybe sleep would help, however he seemed to toss and turn for that entire hour, not getting thoughts of Jillian out of his head.

But there were also visions of Dorian and Sindra and Stan and his parents and the other businesses on his street in Acorn Hills. There were people chasing him who seemed to want to hurt him. He heard himself almost yelling "Enough!" and heaved a sigh that started another coughing spell. Okay, he could do this. He could do this presentation and hop back on the plane tonight and be home in his own bed, well, the bed at the office anyway, within 24 hrs. He forced himself to get up, brushed his teeth and hair, finished dressing, called the front desk for the limo that was at his disposal to take him to and from the meetings, walked to the door and closed it behind him.

Tomeiki, Ltd. was the mirror twin of Evans Enterprises in this part of Japan. The state of the art building was a modern art lover's dream. The angles, the reflective glass, the furnishings….no expense had been spared. Ando Tomeiki WAS Jake Evans in a foreign land. When the two were introduced, they bowed and shook hands and Ando invited Jake into the board room where ten others were seated around a massive walnut table.

"Mr. Evans, so good having you with us," Ando began. "Please, begin when you are ready. We are most anxious to hear what you have brought to us." Tomeike gestured with his hand for Jake to stand and begin his presentation.

Jake thought to himself as he listened and watched the animations in Ando Tomeiki's introduction of him that he looked like the moderator of the television program "Iron Chef". He wrinkled his brow. Why was his head thinking of so many weird trivial things? From Jillian to Dorian; his parents to crazy television programs...none of it made sense to him. It was like a life review was happening all garbled up in his brain and in front of his eyes, and he wasn't quite sure why. He pushed these thoughts out of his head and forced himself to focus on the task at hand.

Ninety minutes after Jake began his presentation he concluded with, "Thank you for this opportunity. And I certainly want you to consider what has been offered. I do not take this venture lightly. We really truly want Tomeiki, Ltd. to be on board with Evans Enterprises to create the best future for us all. Thank you." He bowed and went back to his seat by Ando Tomeiki.

Ando rose and addressed the others "We have much to deliberate, Mr. Evans. You have given us much to think on. I assure you an answer will come within the week." He bowed to Jake again and Jake took that as his sign of dismissal and rose and walked from the board room.

The limo driver was waiting for him in the lobby and had seen to it that his luggage had been packed up and placed in the limo awaiting the drive to the airport. There was no over-night, no time to explore or play.

Jake thought humph...doesn't take them long to do things...in...out...over. He chuckled. Kind of like how it was with Dorian. He chuckled again. He noticed the look from the limo driver in the rearview mirror and just smiled.

Thankfully the airport was only minutes away, and if the flight was on time, he would be taking off for home in no time. The limo driver waited by the door as Jake took his luggage pausing long enough to give the driver a generous tip before plunging into the throngs of travelers at the airport as part of his journey through the tunnels of people to the right gate.

Jake was thankful for the moving sidewalks inside the airport. He was tired—so very tired--and just wanted to get to his destination and sleep. Somewhere in one of the stores that lined the moving path came the most disgusting smell, some sort of acrid incense or something. It was enough to get Jake coughing again and coughing hard.

Blood ran from his mouth down his chin and the violent coughing and gagging continued. Suddenly everything was moving slower as the corners of his vision faded, then the sides and then everything was becoming black as if looking through a pin hole. Jake fell, blood running from his mouth. He laid motionless on the moving sidewalk as hundreds of other travelers started screaming and yelling, their voices falling into silence as they tried to get someone to come to his aid.

    A group of American students surrounded Jake. One ran down the moving sidewalk, pushing people out of the way, to where the security booth was to get them to stop the sidewalk so someone could attend to this man who was unconscious and bleeding profusely. The teen asked the security guard to call 911 and when he didn't understand, he grabbed the phone and did it himself. The other students could only stay by Jake's side until help came.

CHAPTER FOURTEEN

For many visitors, Acorn Hills State Park was the most beautiful park in the state. There were acres of wildflowers exploding in wild bursts of yellow, purple, white, and gold across a natural canvas where an occasional deer was seen munching. Picnic areas with small shelter houses dotted the entire acreage allowing full enjoyment of the site from spring bloom to the fall leaves. The park boasted a wide range of hiking and bicycling trails of all levels of difficulty, from pure novice to experienced outdoor specialist, as well as a sand beach and swimming area.

But what it was best known for was the calm waters for boaters. The lake was fed from rivers and streams from the high country of the Cascades. The pristine surroundings were being found by many outsiders who were buying up lakeside property to build their "get-away" dream homes, leaving all too little public land left.

Fortunately for everyone who enjoyed this park, a trust that had been set up by several well-to-do families in Acorn Hills. It specified that this certain portion of land could never be sold to private individuals and that it was to remain for all of those who came into the park to enjoy. Granted, it was a state park and required a lot of care, but the state took pride in its parks and the monies from the trust helped greatly when it came to upkeep on restrooms and other things.

Richard was packing up the final supplies in the Blazer and checking the boat multiple times to make sure it was all secure. He was glad he made the decision to keep the SUV to haul the boat. He could hook it up to the Nitro, but the memories tied to the Blazer went back to when he and his dad went fishing. So every time he hooked up the boat to the old vehicle, he felt the presence of his dad.

He wistfully looked up, "Dad, I don't know what I'm doing here. I'm gonna need your guidance with this one."

Richard was looking forward to getting away for the day. Who was he kidding? He was looking forward to a day with Jillian. Truly they both needed it; and he was thinking the other four did, too, by the way they jumped on his invitation. He walked back into the kitchen making sure he didn't forget anything. He checked his watch and picked up the phone. It didn't even ring one time before she answered it.

"Jilly…it's Richard. I'm just calling to make sure you'll be ready when I get there." He smiled.

"Yes, I'm ready now, actually. I got things together last night and made some brownies and other things,' Jillian said.

"Always could count on you to supply the neighborhood with food. Girl, you'd think you were cooking for an army!" They both laughed simultaneously.

"Well," Jillian began, "you never know how much David or Jordan will eat, not to mention YOU." She put special emphasis on the last word. He could feel the smile in her voice and that made him smile.

"Sure, blame me!" He continued to tease "I am going to gain 20 pounds today just because of you and David! He seemed to think he needed to bring things to eat too! I just finished putting the last stuff in the Blazer so I'll be over to get you in about 15 minutes. Will that work?"

"Not a problem, Richard. As I said, I'm ready to roll." There was true excitement in her voice and that made him happy. "Are the others meeting us there or are we picking them up too?" she inquired.

"Well, we need to have 2 vehicles for all the food and other gear. I think Ginger and Jordan are bringing the canoes, so everything but you and what you are bringing rides with them. David and Denise are over at their place with all the stuff they are bringing." Richard explained." They should be here any minute."

"Great! See you all soon" Jillian responded and placed her cell phone back in her pocket.

Jillian was smiling. For the first time in weeks she actually felt happy. A day away doing something she really enjoyed with people she loved was just what the doctor ordered! She knew it had been way too long since she had given herself the relaxing reward of a day of play. Alex told her that he would take care of the shop. It was Sunday and if one of the funeral homes called he would let her know.

She was so thankful for her older son. The boys had been her rock when their dad died. They all became closer than they ever had been before and Alex stepped up into the role of caregiver to his mother. It seemed something he truly wanted to do and Jillian was glad she had Alex to depend on. There were days that she hated the loneliness, that feeling of emptiness and having Alex close helped with that. She knew at some point he was going to start his life, at least she hoped he would do that soon, but for now, things were working well and it felt like things were as they should be. It was still a bitter pill to swallow. Jillian still wasn't ready to deal with Brett's death.

As always Richard was right on time; fifteen minutes later and he was knocking on the door. He was always prompt, always kept his word. You never had to guess about anything with Richard. He gave her a hurried hug hello and kissed her cheek. She saw David and Denise in the back seat of the Suburban.

"Let's get movin, girl!" he said as he grabbed the two bags on the floor. Jillian rolled her eyes and threw her purse over her shoulder, grabbed the food from the kitchen counter, and her keys and out the door they flew.

Jillian giggled, remembering hustling out the door with an arm load of books on the many mornings that Ginger's mom had stopped to pick her up for school. She loved these friends so much. They were all family. They WERE connected on a level that no one else seemed to understand and she truly couldn't imagine life without them around her.

The day was calm, not even a hint of a slight breeze to disturb the water, and the completely calm and clear water of Acorn Lake was reflecting the crystal blue of the sky. The pontoon lazily cruised to the middle of the lake before Richard stopped the engine and anchored.

Hours passed as they laughed and ate and reminisced about growing up together.

"Oh, Lord, we all have come so far over the years" Ginger stated as she stuffed a piece of watermelon in her mouth.

"I'll say. When Richard picked me up and hurried me out the door," Jillian gave him the raised eyebrow and continued. "It reminded me so much of those mornings Ginger, when your mom would stop the bus in front of my house and I would go running out the door with the camera bag over one shoulder, my back pack over the other one and an arm full of books."

"Those huge rose colored frog eyed glasses you wore and those bell bottom jeans and fringe vests," Ginger was laughing so hard she was snorting.

"And, let's not forget those Birkenstocks" Richard added.

"Denise, I think you and I missed out on a lot. Maybe we were better for not being with this rowdy bunch, ya think?" Jordan put his arm around Denise.

"Trust me, we really didn't do much. We were all so involved in shit at school that the only times we communicated were at sporting events because Ginger was cheerleader-dance queen and Jillian was the photographer for the journalism class." Richard explained.

"Well, yeah, and then there is you, Mr. Hotshot-athlete-who-had-to-be-in- every-freaking-sport there was." Jillian shoulder chucked Richard.

David grabbed one of the stuffed mushrooms and popped it in his mouth. "Hell, I was so out of it most days that I don't remember much of high school. I was high all the time. I think that is why my parents decided I was going into the Navy upon graduation."

"Well, I am just glad that you and I got to be together in that hell hole Nam." Richard patted David on the back. "There were days that thoughts of you guys, of Jillian looking at me over the fence with that brace clad smile, and you, Ginger cheering at all the Jr. High games, that is what got me through; not to mention having David by my side." Richard's eyes misted. "Yes, we all have been through so much."

Jordan raised his glass, "To friends who stay forever and for friendships that never die. Skol!" Everyone met his glass in the middle of their circle and touched each other's, cementing this lifelong journey they all were on.

"You know, David, one of the memories that sticks in my head to this day is you dressed in a plaid skirt with a baseball hat and black rimmed glasses sitting on the toilet. I think one of your front teeth was blacked out even." Jillian slyly smiled.

"HEY! That was a very private moment. Here we are trying to practice for the stinking senior play, and I can't even remember what the name of the damn thing was. But I had to dress up as this geek in a skirt. I hid in the bathroom because I didn't want anyone seeing me…but…I hid in the girls' bathroom, not the boys. I realized that when Marcia Burke and Wendy Thornson walked in." David chuckled. "I knew I had better just stay where I was because if the teachers found out I was in there I was going to be tossed out of school on my ass for sure. Then those girls left and here comes Patsy the Photographer. Somehow, she knew I was hiding in there. She opened the stall door and there was a flash and now I am a permanent memory in the year book!"

By this point in the story Richard was laughing so hard tears were rolling down his cheeks. He had never confessed to David that HE was the one who set him up for that photo. Patsy was such a good sport.

David put his arm around Denise knowing how difficult all this must be for her. He placed a kiss on her cheek and whispered in her ear "I love you, Sweetheart." She looked at him and kissed his mouth and whispered back, "thank you."

"Denise, I hope all this reminiscing isn't making you too upset." Ginger put her hand on Denise's shoulder. Leave it to Ginger to speak her mind.

"No, it is fine. It is so much fun to hear about all of this stuff. More than that is to hear of the happy stuff and the fun stuff that you all were involved in." Denise smiled at her friend.

"I know what you went through back then. It isn't easy being bullied at school and then to go home to what you had to go home to. I am so glad someone noticed before you were hurt worse than you were." Jillian's voice soft with concern.

"I owe a lot of my safety to your parents, JuJu. Had it not been for your Dad getting me out of that house, I'd be dead." Denise confessed. "But that was a long time ago and many counseling sessions ago and I am not that person."

"No, my darling, you aren't." David hugged her and kissed her again.

The sun felt good as they sat and told stories but it was getting higher in the sky and the temperatures were increasing as well. Everyone had their swimsuits on under big shirts and shorts.

Ginger and Jordan decided to jump from the boat into the lake for a swim, yelling for the others to join them.

"C'mon you guys," Jordan urged.

David and Denise followed shortly thereafter. The foursome chased each other, dipping under the water and popping up behind someone else only to dunk them under. They were laughing so much it made Richard laugh, too, as he watched their antics.

"So, Jilly, wanna join them?" Richard asked as he nodded his head toward the others. He was already shirtless and in his swim trunks.

"Richard, if you'd like to join them, go for it. I think I just want to hang out here in the sun, in the peace and quiet of this glorious summer day." Jillian tossed her head back and looked up so the sun shone fully on her face.

"Trust me, I won't be bored. I", she emphasized, "brought a book." She replied holding up a book and flashed him a cheesy grin, quickly raising and lowering her eyebrows.

"Jilly," Richard began, as he raised his left eyebrow then continued. "I am worried about you. You don't eat, you look like you haven't slept in weeks, and you have this propensity for being alone. Please talk to me. What's going on, honey?" Richard put his hand on her arm.

Jillian looked up into Richard's face, into his expressive, tender chocolate eyes and felt the tears pour out as she began crying without warning. Immediately Richard's arms were around her and his hands smoothing her hair and soothing her sorrow. "Honey, what is going on? What has you this upset?"

Jillian felt her chest heave and shoulders shudder as she sobbed, truly sobbed, for the first time since ending things with Jake. Her heart hurt so much! She couldn't accept the other women; she couldn't understand how he could be so cold, so cruel to her.

She didn't know why she wasn't enough for him. She hated to voice how she was feeling. God, what would Richard think if she just blurted out what was making her so upset? Richard was her best male friend. He had always been there, always soothed her emotionally when things weren't right. She trusted him and she so wanted to just get all this out so she didn't have to deal with it alone. She was glad the others were out in the water away from them so she could let go, so she could share with her best friend what was going on.

"Richard, I'm never enough. Never! I give all of who I am, I hold nothing back. I don't lie, cheat or steal" she sobbed. "What is wrong with me? Why did Jake have to do what he did? Why did he have to have others? Why am I never enough?" the tears came faster the harder she cried.

Richard found himself at a loss for words. He remembered asking his dad for help with this and he was silently waiting for a sign or a verbal word of some kind but nothing came. He was on his own with this one. He could console Marines who had lost limbs. He could comfort parents who had lost their child. But what he couldn't do was see Jillian hurting like this and not know what to do or say to make it stop. That just killed him inside.

He noticed David climbing up the steps to get back into the boat and because Jillian's back was to them, he shooed David back down and the others followed, swimming back out away from the pontoon. He would clue them in later, maybe.

All he could do was sit there with this beautiful woman in his arms and hold her as she fell apart. He couldn't talk. Hell, he couldn't even think with Jillian this close to him. All of the old feelings he had for her flooded his mind, his heart, his soul.

I'll kill him for hurting her so badly, he thought. Time stopped, his arms froze around Jillian and his hands stroked her silky hair. For a moment he was transported back to the day at the airport; the day he left for the Navy. Jillian and her family and several others went to "see him off". He almost got on the plane, but turned around in time for her to fly at him with a huge hug. She was so young, yet that hug meant more to him than anything at that moment.

He loosened his hold on her and grabbed her face with both hands, his thumbs wiping away the tears that ran down her cheeks, her chin.

"You listen to me, Jilly, you listen!" He commanded as he searched her face, looked into her eyes and softened his expression. "Honey, don't let me ever, and I mean EVER hear you say you are not enough. You are so enough and then some! Jake, he is just a good for nothing son-of-a-bitch who took advantage of you, of what you offered him. He played on your goodness and took from you what HE wanted. He took from you the positive energy you gave. He took the love you offered him and blew the smoke screen around you to make you think he truly cared about you.

"He took from you the hospitality you gave. He took from you the majority of YOU! He is a player, Jilly, a player. And I am so proud of you for getting out from under his bullshit." Richard pulled her closer to him.

Jillian rested her head on his shoulder, and somehow at that very moment she knew in her heart of hearts everything was going to be alright. She knew that she would get over Jake and that the hurt would end…at some point. She knew that she was going to be able to trust again, but it wouldn't be soon. She knew that if she could just hold on to what she believed; trust her faith, trust that still, small, internal voice, she truly would be alright. Wouldn't she?

CHAPTER FIFTEEN

As the sun began to set on Acorn Lake, painting the water with its golden reflection, the group came to a begrudging consensus that they better pack things up and get off the lake before there was no sunlight left at all. They stood together as a happy group, arm in arm on the deck of the pontoon and watched the sun as it seemed to be diving into the lake. The vivid sky of pinks and oranges quickly turned to muted shades of violet and mauve. A worthy ending for what felt like such a perfect day.

The girls spent their time packing up the leftovers while the guys readied the pontoon to go back on to the trailer of Richard's vehicle. David helped Jordan load their vehicle as well. They didn't even use the canoes, but it was a good idea to have had them along anyway. Better to have and not need than to need and not have. Jordan said that they were going to stay loaded that maybe the four of them could go out some evening after work if the weather was good and David was all for that.

Everyone gave hugs to one another and bid their farewells, saying again what a rich time it was and that they needed to do it more often. Jordan pulled away from where the Blazer was parked and they all waved. Jillian sighed, her heart still heavy from the conversation from earlier.

"Ready?" the sound of Richard's voice brought her back to present time. She nodded as he helped her up into the seat then buckled her seatbelt and shut her door like a true gentleman. He walked around the back of the Blazer checking one more time that all was secure and climbed in the driver's seat and headed for home.

The trip home was quiet in an eerie awkward sort of way. Richard didn't know whether he should talk or just leave it alone. He found a light jazz channel on the radio, perfect soothing background music for silence or for conversation. Jillian's thoughts wandered back to earlier in the day.

Following the "meltdown" she decided that maybe a swim wouldn't be such a bad thing after all, so she and Richard joined the others in the water for over an hour. It felt so good, so natural to be back with these wonderful people who meant so much to her throughout her life. For some reason when she and Jake were together, there was very little socializing with others, unless it was at corporate dinners or meetings.

They were always together, but never with anyone else. It was one late night business meeting after another or dinner parties where she served as "knowledgeable eye candy" on Jake's arm. Even though there were other people around, they were a lone duo. Jake always said "I am with people all day, why do I want to be with people after I get off work? I don't need to be anywhere but home. I don't need anyone but you." What a lie!

She sighed not realizing it was out loud until she felt Richard's hand covering hers in an "I'm here for you" kind of way. It was comforting to know he cared. She covered his hand with her other one and just squeezed and let go. How could she feel so empty, so lifeless after a day like today? Just a few minutes with her own thoughts, and here she was in that old empty chasm yet again.

It was nearly midnight when Richard dropped Jillian off from their lake outing. Upon reaching Jillian's driveway, Richard turned off the ignition and sat in quiet for a few moments before moving. He knew if he didn't get out of the vehicle he was going to do something that neither of them was ready for.

Richard wanted so desperately to hold Jillian and kiss her senseless. He had wanted to do that all day. But there was no way he was going to take advantage of her, especially with what was going on in her head and in her heart. She was vulnerable, and even if there was a remote possibility that she did have feelings for him, deep down he knew he'd still be taking advantage of her if he made his move during this mess. He held the door open for her and helped her out of the Blazer.

He walked her up to the door, took her keys and unlocked it.

"Remember, Jilly," Richard began as he tightly hugged her. "You ARE enough. You always have been and you always will be. I am only a phone call away." He released her from the hug, but kept his hands on her shoulders. He kissed her cheek and squeezed her again and then off he went. Jillian stood at the door waving, wondering when or if they would ever all be together again.

Jillian opened the door and flicked on the foyer light. She reached down and untied her shoes, took them off and placed them on the shoe caddy near the door. Damn! She forgot to get the dishes and things from Richard's vehicle. She shrugged. She would just stop by the store tomorrow and get them.

Knowing Richard as she did, they would be emptied and cleaned and in a sack when she got there. She shook her head and smiled as she made her way to the living room, turning on lights and turning off others as she went. Richard. She smiled. Richard was something else. Richard was so kind and so sweet and so tender to her and had been for as long as she could remember.

It had been difficult yet joyful growing up next door to Richard. He and Chris, Jillian's older brother, were friends in high school, so she became "just the annoying little sister." When the guys got together for a game of touch football in the Dempsey's back yard, she was right there wanting to be a part of it. Chris always shooed her away and told her to go home. Richard always included her on his team and often gave her the ball to run. Since she was smaller and faster than most of the guys she gladly took the ball and ran. Her brace-clad smile was bright enough to light the sky and it always made Richard smile at her and reward her with a "good job Jilly". Even when Richard left for Nam he hugged her and told her to study hard and not give up. He always gave her hope, which was something that was sorely lacking between her and her brother.

Why couldn't Jake be more like Richard? She sat down on the couch and put her feet on the glass topped coffee table. She sighed. Oh, God, how did she get into such messes? How was it that she seemed to attract every stray that needed something instead of meeting the Prince Charming she deserved? She was so good at giving she never held anything in reserve for herself. And therein lay the number one problem. Note to self: Always keep a part of me for ME.

She looked at the clock on the fireplace mantle. It was 12:48 a.m. She needed to get some sleep. Tomorrow was Monday and she needed to be fresh for work. She sighed again. Getting up from the couch she stretched and in mid yawn her cell phone rang.

Jillian stared at her phone. This couldn't be good. After college no one ever called at 12:48 a.m. without it being bad news. Jillian pulled her cell phone from her pocket and looked at the caller ID but didn't recognize the number. She rolled her eyes. It was probably someone drunk dialing her. She shrugged and shook her head. The phone kept ringing. It would go to voicemail and then stop for a moment and ring again. "Alright already!" she said aloud and finally answered it despite her shaking hands.

"Hello?" Jillian answered tentatively.

"Jillian? Thank God I reached you! This is Joni; Jake's secretary." The voice on the other end of the phone was definitely shaken.

"Joni, what is going on? It is nearly 1 a.m." Jillian's heart pounded faster as she spoke.

"Jillian," Joni choked up, "I don't know how to say this so I just am going to say it. Jake never made his flight home. Andy and I were to have picked him up from the airport today. I phoned Mr. Tomeiki this afternoon. I have been trying to reach you all day. I left you several messages. Didn't you get them? I got your cell number from the office, from that address roll thing in Jake's office. This is just unreal." Joni rambled on.

Jillian wanted to know what was happening to make her be so scattered like this. Joni was usually a very cool, very calm person. It was really strange for her to sound so shaken. Joni was usually the rock everyone depended on for everything at work and at home.

"Joni, I've been out at the lake all day, I just got home. Now what is this nonsense about Jake not making his flight? He is always on time when he travels. I bet you anything he is in some Japanese hotel room with some hot little native or stewardess he keeps on staff." Jillian assured her.

"Jillian, you don't understand, he's gone. I mean, I talked to Mr. Tomeiki. Jake was taken to a Tokyo hospital because he was coughing up massive amounts of blood. He slipped into a coma and….and…" Joni started crying again. "Jillian, he died this afternoon."

The words hung in the air like stagnant cigar smoke. Jillian pulled the cell phone from her ear and just looked at it. No, that couldn't be right! This was some type of sick prank Jake was playing, so he could screw someone new. There was no way Jake could be dead. She would feel it…wouldn't she? Reason and adrenaline took over at that point and she put the phone back to her ear.

"Joni, I will be at your house in 20 minutes." Jillian disconnected the call, slipped into her shoes without tying them and grabbed her keys. She was going to get to the bottom of this, RIGHT NOW!

There was an eerie quiet as she traveled through blinking yellow traffic lights and then the dark side streets to Joni's house. The traffic was minimal and she hit all the traffic lights that weren't blinking when they were green, and that was a feat in itself, even on a good day. She knew she was speeding, but at this point she didn't care, she needed to find out what the hell was going on.

Jillian pulled up in Joni's driveway and turned off the ignition, bounded out of the vehicle and before she could even knock on the door, it was already opened. Joni was standing there, mascara running down a tear stained face, Andy's arm was around his wife's shoulders and they solemnly invited her into the house so Joni could tell her all the news she had about Jake.

"And, that's all I know, Jillian." Joni wiped the tears from her cheeks. She had just told Jillian that Jake had done a great statistical presentation of why Evans needed this holding.

Mr. Tomeiki had told her that he was impressed with the presentation and would get back to him. Jake arrived at the airport, collapsed on the moving sidewalk, and was taken to a Tokyo hospital. As much as the medical staff tried, they could not revive him. He had lost too much blood. Although there was going to be an autopsy to determine the exact cause of death, the preliminary diagnosis was a fatal aortic abdominal aneurism. No other information was given, and this was all 3rd hand now to Jillian...from the hospital staff to Tomeiki and from Tomeiki to Joni and now from Joni to her.

Jake had no living relatives. He was alone, except for her and he didn't even have that when he died. He died in a foreign land. He died alone. That thought bothered her more than the fact that he was gone. What type of cruel, heartless bitch had she become? She couldn't even cry about this.

An overwhelming sadness washed over her as she sat there on Joni's couch with her by her side and Andy with an arm around Jillian and holding his wife's hand at the same time. She stared ahead in disbelief, hearing what Joni had said, yet feeling like she was in some bad horror flick, knowing as soon as the credits were rolled, the lights would go up and things would be alright. Yet a part deep in her soul knew that it wasn't ever going to be alright. There wasn't going to be any reunion, no growth, no apology and no closure. Jake was gone, just like that, and there was no way to say anything that was still left to be said.

Joni was a mess. Her husband was trying to console her. And here she sat, emotionless, trying to process the news that she had just heard. She didn't even get to say good bye. She really didn't know what to do, what to feel, how to react. She was numb. Why weren't there tears? Why wasn't she hysterical about all of this? Jake dead? Really?

CHAPTER SIXTEEN

Frantic panic hit Denise like a ton of bricks. She still couldn't believe that she had successfully dealt with the Italian pain in the ass and that the company shipped her original order overnight.

Denise spent the better part of the past twenty four hours finalizing models, making sure that each piece of delicate lingerie looked its best and stocked the tables with several copies of the books and other products Sultry Sensations carried. If she wasn't ready now, she never would be. The tables were covered with informational and promotional material. She made sure that it was a good mix of what she offered and the information Gwendolyn had provided her on Multiple Sclerosis. Just because you had this disease, didn't mean that you couldn't look fabulous, regardless of the stage of disability.

The ground floor banquet room at the Oakdale Regency Hotel filled with laughter as women of all ages gathered for the Governor's wife's benefit for Multiple Sclerosis. Gwendolyn Sutter, wife of the state's most honored man, Governor Mike Sutter, was diagnosed with the disease in her early thirties. Since that time she had become an avid spokesperson for Multiple Sclerosis and last year began the "Get Moving Now" benefit that brought many people and many substantial givers from all corners of the state.

Gwendolyn was a tall, stately woman and did not look anywhere near her sixty years of age. Her three daughters and eight grandchildren were by her side at most MS functions, and when Mike could join her he usually did. However, this was a "girls' night out" only. Young and old from all walks of society were truly enjoying the opportunity to make new friends, renew old friendships, and browse the items that were on display. And many were dropping big bucks on products as well as making generous donations to fund MS research at the local level.

Dr. Rosaline Burdock, head of the neurology department of the local hospital opened the event. "Ladies, I cannot thank you enough for coming out to support this event and Gwendolyn and our fight to find a cure for Multiple Sclerosis.

"Over 400,000 people in the US alone, of all ages suffer from the effects of MS. As you know, MS affects everyone differently. For those of you who are new to this disease, either as a care giver, a victim, or a supporter; MS is an auto-immune disease and a disease where the body attacks itself. Rogue cells that begin as good immune cells begin seeing different things in the MS affected body as foreign material. In doing so, they eat away the covering of the nerves causing a short circuiting from the brain as it sends signals to the different body parts.

"We are so close to unraveling the cause and cure for this and many other neurological and neuro-muscular auto-immune diseases. If you are interested in knowing more details, I will be here all night and would love to answer any questions you may have that would help you understand it better. This night is for fun. It is for discovery. It is for raising the roof on research. Thank you again for your part in all of this. Thank you for your support of the products that are displayed and the vendors who took time to set up such a great variety. More than anything, I personally thank you for standing behind research. We are so close, ladies, so close to helping those of you here with MS and the future generations."

Dr. Burdock's short message touched the hearts of many in the room and was met with polite but enthusiastic applause. This was the first indicator that these women were not afraid to give and give from their hearts.

The first hour of the fund raiser was sponsored by the owners of the Acorn Hills winery. Bud and Roxie had won countless international awards. They brought bottles of all of their wines to sample, purchase and/or order. A delectable meal of seafood, salads and desserts was served and topped off with several different coffees by the city's best baristas. All of them were being cheered on, of course, for the different foam images on the tops of the frothy beverages.

Almost as soon as dinner began, or so it seemed, the servers were sweeping away the remnants and getting the room ready for the auction of the lingerie, the most important part of the entire evening. While this was going on, the women browsed the tables, bought glasses of wine and visited with the vendors.

"Ladies, if you would take your seats again, please." Gwendolyn began. She waited until most were seated and continued. "We have such a treat tonight. I want to introduce to you a dear girl, Denise Berrie, the owner of

Sultry Sensations."

The introduction was paused for a moment as the crowd applauded politely once again. "Denise supported my whim to have an auction of imported lingerie as part of our fundraiser this year. She worked tireless hours to get this together for me and for that I am so thankful. Denise, where are you?" She shaded her eyes and looked out into the crowd.

Denise stood and waved, the applause and whistles and cheers warmed her heart. Gwendolyn Sutter continued. "Following the auction, Denise will be here to answer any questions you may have about your purchases or about any of the products you see on her tables, and I'm sure she'll answer any questions you have on ideas to really get your fella's attention next Valentine's Day." The audience laughed appreciatively.

"Ladies, shall we get started?" The first model made her way through the crowd, walking up and down the aisles as Gwendolyn Sutter described the ecru Italian satin baby doll.

Bidding began at $500. Denise found she had to close her open mouth to hide her shock! Item after item was paraded through the throng of excited women who were not afraid to voice their opinions on what they saw by the increasingly higher amounts that were bid.

There was not one item that didn't bring a hefty bid and most brought out some friendly bid-bantering. The final lingerie item was what Denise thought the best of the best. It was a floor length spaghetti strap aquamarine satin, slit to the hip on the right side. There was a diamond-shaped lace cut out that revealed the model's navel. The back dipped very low. "Ladies, what man could resist you if you were slowly walking toward him in this lovely piece?" Gwendolyn asked.

Denise noticed that Mrs. Sutter was sounding pretty tired at this point and that made her realize that she was kind of getting that way herself. She let her mind wander a bit as she looked around the room. She was aware of voices still bidding on this final item and tried to keep at least one ear tuned to what was being said.

The gavel hit the podium with a hearty "SOLD!" The sharp rap of the gavel caused Denise to jump out of her trance. The piece sold for $23,567.00. The room erupted with applause and instead of dismissing the crowd, Mrs. Sutter, with the aid of one of her daughters stepped away from where she had been standing and sat down at the table that was in front of the podium. It was time to let the ladies take over the rest of the evening.

Denise quickly made her way to her area. She smiled as she proudly looked around at several tables that held an assortment of what she sold at Sultry Sensations. As the women continued visiting and comparing the lingerie that was now theirs, she noted how varied her audience was and how pleased she was with herself that she had pulled a variety of products everyone seemed to like. There were items for the naïve as well as the most sexually experienced woman who wanted to bring more excitement to her relationships. There were "how to" books, there were fragrances to sample as well as taste, there were countless vibrators in a rainbow of colors, and feathers and other toys to enhance pleasure, not to mention the beautiful imported Italian lingerie that finally arrived just in the nick of time!

Denise surveyed what was going on. Yes, this was a huge success and the single most lucrative day/evening her business had ever seen. In fact, it blew her wildest dreams for the night away. She promised Gwendolyn she would stay for the first hour following the auction to answer questions, do demonstrations (if needed, within reason!) and just mingle. The hour passed as did the next 2! These women were crazy! They were fun! Most had returned to the wine bar and held a glass in one hand and their purchases tucked under the other arm. The best part; they knew what pleasure and being sensual were all about. Finally, people who truly did appreciate her and her business! Denise surprised even herself and stayed until the last person left.

She stood by the table just inside the door, the one that held the "how to" books, when Mrs. Sutter came up to her. "Denise!" Gwendolyn extended her arm for a hug then put it around her new friend's waist. "You have totally exceeded my expectations with all of the things you've done to make this such a successful event. I cannot thank you enough!"

"Mrs. Sutter, I'm so glad things turned out so well. Looks like you had an amazing response to your personal invites and I'm honored that you even took a chance with me, with my business. It is I who should be thanking you for this wonderful opportunity!" Denise beamed.

Gwendolyn gently hugged Denise again, but didn't stay there for long. Being the wife of Mike Sutter afforded her the luxury of using one of her most charming gifts, that of a wonderful conversationalist. Mingling was not difficult for her. She moved from one little gathering to another, shaking hands, giving hugs; thanking everyone for their generosity.

All evening it seemed there were little groups of two to five women scattered across the room. Some were noshing on the finger foods, some were just talking, and others were still perusing the tables trying to figure out what to buy. Out of the corner of her eye, Denise spotted an elegantly dressed older woman at one of her tables, picking up different things then putting them down.

Denise walked over to the woman and extended her hand. "Hi. My name is Denise and I own Sultry Sensations. Do you have any questions I can help you with?" She could tell the woman was a bit distraught, but couldn't discern if it was because she was just confused as to what to do with what she was looking at or if it all was very disgusting to her.

"Oh, dear!" the woman exclaimed. "I don't know where or how to begin."

Denise could tell how nervous this woman was and tried to put her at ease by just talking openly with her. "Well, I am here to answer your questions. There is nothing to be afraid of, trust me. When I began this shop, I wanted it to be a place where women could come to openly explore their sexual and sensual sides without worrying about what anyone else may say or think. I read a lot, played with a lot, so I got to know the products that I wanted to sell and got rid of those I didn't feel were a good idea. So, please, don't be embarrassed. Feel free to ask me anything. If I don't know the answer, I certainly will get it for you when I go back to the shop and make sure it gets in your hands." She placed her hand on the older woman's shoulder in a reassuring gesture.

"Denise, my granddaughter thinks I need to explore what makes me "feel" good. I was married to my dear Everett for 53 years and not once did we ever have problems pleasing each other. Everett passed on, and after having such an active sex life, I am missing the things Everett and I shared. My granddaughter, cheeky thing she be, said 'Grandma, you need a vibrator'." The older woman's cheeks pinked a bit. 'It will help when you think of what you shared with Grandpa and how much you loved being together,' she told me. Frankly, I think she needs to mind her own business", she chuckled, "but then when Gwendolyn told me about this fundraiser, I started thinking it was about time to get educated."

She and Denise both laughed. Denise put her hand on the woman's elbow and led her to the table with a wide array of vibrators; pink ones, purple ones, ones that rotated, ones that had different speeds. And she began to pick them up one at a time and show the product and what it had to offer and how to work it. The 'seventy-something' woman was very attentive and decided on the 'perfect' product to start her adventure of pleasing herself as she thought of her dear Everett.

Denise put her purchase in the glitzy black and silver Sultry Sensations bag and handed it to her. She noticed the crowd had thinned and there were very few people left. All of the lingerie sold at auction. Her tables were very picked over and she was elated that so many purchased her products, but more than that was the one on one contact and networking she did. She ran out of business cards, it was a great feeling.

The colorful cardboard displays were folded flat and Denise began packing the remainder of things into their travel tubs. She loaded the tubs onto the luggage dolly and began rolling it toward the door and ultimately to her vehicle. Gwendolyn was standing by the door, actually leaning against the doorframe.

"Gwendolyn, thank you so much for this opportunity," Denise hugged her. "I know you have to be so exhausted. Please know that 10% of my take tonight will go as my donation to this fundraiser. And, it goes without saying, if there is anything I can do for you, personally, at any time, I am only a phone call away."

"Denise, I can't thank you enough for such a wonderful evening! I hope we can make this an annual event. I saw you spent quite a lot of time with Emma Swopes…and I saw that she left with a glitter bag. Some day you will have to tell me that story."

Gwendolyn chuckled and switched topics. "Yes, I am exhausted. Mike just called to say that he was sending a car for me." She hugged Denise. "I know you will be a huge success here in Acorn Hills and statewide. I have your business card and again, thank you for everything. I will call you next week."

Governor Sutter arrived, greeted Denise then quickly ushered his wife from the venue into their chauffeur driven vehicle. Denise made a couple trips back into the hotel to make sure she hadn't left something behind.

A broad smile crossed her face, brightening her tired eyes. She couldn't wait to get home and tell David about what had happened today.

CHAPTER SEVENTEEN

Richard took his glasses off and laid them on top of the mound of invoices in front of him and rubbed his tired eyes. He glanced up at the clock. It was already 1 a.m. He had been working on checking in all the new merchandise, making sure the order was complete, making sure he didn't get something he didn't want. Sometimes owning a business when the "buck stopped here" was exhausting. He leaned back in the old office chair and looked around.

There was so much that needed to be cleaned, filed and tossed, including the chair he was sitting in. As a young boy, back when he worked for Roy after school and on weekends, Richard remembered seeing him tilting back in the chair when he was talking on the phone, and those memories are precisely why the chair still had residence in his office.

Going through the mounds of papers was something he had been working on since he purchased the business. The Braxtons had kept every receipt from every purchase from the inception of the store but they were here and there and tossed in with other papers and he couldn't find anything when he started this adventure. Adventure. He smiled. Yes, it certainly had been an adventure. If anyone would have told him seven years ago at the age of fifty five he would be the owner of his own antique store, and a very successful one at that, he would have told them to cut back on whatever it was they were smoking! There was no way!

Richard had really hoped that at this stage of his life, he would be bouncing grand babies on his lap, traveling with the love of his life, living the "good life". Someone evidently had different plans for him. He just wished that that someone would enlighten him as to what path to travel down next.

Tonight was much the same as most of the others. He found he would rather spend time at the store than in his empty house. It kept his mind occupied and he WAS being productive. Sleep evaded him most nights anyway, and lately when he did get to sleep the flashbacks from Nam plagued him. Strange how those would come and go over the years, and they came in full fearful force every time now and he would wake up drenched in sweat, re-living every moment of every year he spent fighting.

So rather than go through that night after night, he came to the store and threw himself into his work. There was certainly a lot that needed doing and he was making strides toward crossing off more things on the "to do" list.

Richard knew the holidays were right around the corner and he was going to have to come up with a plan for rearranging the entire store and decorating for the Thanksgiving/Christmas season. Even though it was only late August, in retail you needed to think three months ahead of time. He added to his "to do" list by writing a reminder to check on the decorations that he had and what needed replacing.

When Halloween approached, you decorated for it late August or the first part of September. With thoughts of Thanksgiving, decorations would go up October 1st. And Christmas, well, let's just say for him Christmas could happen all year round! He loved the holidays, always had, since he was a little boy.

The fondest memories he had were those of his sister and mother taking out the decorations and hanging them on the huge fresh evergreen tree that he and his dad would bring home. The smell of cinnamon cookies filled his nostrils and he closed his eyes and allowed nostalgia to take him to a more gentle time before the harsh realities of life and of Viet Name came crashing into his innocent world view. Laughter filled the house as relatives and friends stopped by, sometimes invited, most of the time not. His mother always had food and drink to share with everyone. He and his sister would scour the house looking for gifts and never be successful in finding them until they appeared under the tree. Maybe that is the reason to this day for his belief in Santa.

It was 3 a.m. the next time he looked at the clock. He decided 2 hours of sort of restful sleep were better than none. Memories of those holidays still ran through his mind and it was tempting to just put his head down on his desk and sleep a while longer. He knew there were other things that needed his attention, but he needed to get up out of the chair and head for home so he could just stretch out.

Slowly Richard stood up and rubbed the back of his neck, grabbed his jacket and keys, turned off the lights and closed and locked his office door. He made his way to the front of the store, making sure the security lights were on and that none needed replacement. After setting the security alarm and exiting and locking his business, he noticed something strange. His eye was drawn across the street. The apartment above the flower shop was lit up.

     Richard checked his watch again. It was 3:15 a.m. He wondered if Jillian had been working up there and just simply forgot to turn off the lights. It just wasn't like her to be so forgetful as to not turn out the lights and she shouldn't be up this time in the morning anyway.

     His "special forces" instincts kicked in and in quick stealth like moves Richard made his way across the street. For a man over sixty he could still move fairly quickly. He put his hand on the door latch and to his surprise, it was open. He cautiously entered the building. The only lights on in the flower shop were the cooler lights enhancing the colors of the flowers and arrangements on the shelves. He continued to carefully wander through the shop, very aware of his surroundings, making sure everything was okay and no one was hiding causing trouble.

     Once he knew it was secure, he went back and locked the front door and walked to the back of the shop where the inside stairs were that went up to the apartment. Fortunately the iron gates that were normally locked were ajar. He stood at the bottom of the dimly lit stairway and heard soft sobs coming from upstairs. Richard took the steps three at a time to get to the source of what he heard.

     Jake, dead. Jillian shook her head. How could that be? How could she not have felt the void in her soul when it happened? Even though she told him to leave, even though he was a womanizing jerk she still had very real, very deep feelings for him. She was still in shock at the news Joni had given her last night. Thankfully she had been so busy with the shop today that she hadn't really given much thought to it until it was time to close.

     She had told her designers to have a good evening, gave her son a hug and turned back to the workroom. She grabbed the broom and dustpan and began sweeping up the mounds of flower petals and greenery, ribbons and wires that had been tossed on the floor as they all created today. Once properly disposed of, she took a look inside the cooler, consolidated buckets of flowers and took the empty ones to the sink to disinfect them and allow them to dry for tomorrow's use.

     She put the half bottle of soda back on the shelf just inside the cooler door, thinking it would make a good breakfast. Because she sent the others home earlier, she had to cash out the day's sales and record some wire service orders. Jillian filled the container on the counter with enclosure card envelopes, stocked the card holders, and made sure the orders were on the board for tomorrow. Well, for later since it already was tomorrow. She sighed.

     After turning off the workroom and showroom lights Jillian made her way upstairs, flicking the switch at the base of the stairs. She really needed to get the apartment whipped into shape. It wasn't that there was much that needed to be done, but enough that kept her procrastinating. If the space was put together the way she wanted it, on nights like this she could just go upstairs and sleep. She didn't sleep at all last night. It was nearly this time yesterday morning when she returned home from Joni's. They discussed arrangements and what should be done and who should take care of it and when she got home she was still so keyed up.

She had made a pot of coffee when she got home from Joni's and attacked the stack of mail that had piled up. She got caught up in some articles and new designs in the trade magazines she subscribed to, anything to get her mind off of the current situation, and before she knew it sun filtered through her living room windows and she realized it was time to get ready for work.

So, she worked the full day and now found herself upstairs at day's end. She really wasn't sure why she just didn't go home. But at this hour, she may as well just stay here. There was a couch she could crash on and get a few hours of sleep before going back downstairs to tackle another day.

Jillian was numb. She really didn't know what her place was now that she had told Jake to get out. You don't throw away years of loving someone or time that you invest in it. Yes, a part of her still loved Jake, the Jake she knew in the beginning…the loving, attentive, caring man who said that he loved her like none other.

One tear escaped her eye and ran down her cheek. She wiped it away with the back of her hand. Things would be so much easier if she could believe that he had never really truly cared for her at all, but she knew that wasn't true and that made it so much harder. She told Joni that she would contact Stan Austin and see what his thoughts were about all of this and get back with her by the end of the week, when Jake's body was to be shipped stateside. Joni had told her that it could take up to a month for the body to make it back because of the international laws, not to mention the autopsy. There was so much to handle that neither one of them knew anything about!

Jillian walked into the spacious living room and lit the candles on the fireplace mantle. She had thought of starting a fire, but at this late hour decided just boosting the thermostat would be better. She looked at the table behind the couch and saw the box that had been there for over a year now. She had a tendency of keeping things in special boxes. This one happened to be wrapped with royal purple plant foil. When she and Ginger were in high school, she started the "purple box".

She had placed all of her most important memories in the purple box and gave specific instructions to Ginger time and again that if anything ever happened to her that box was to be burned! She had gone through several purple boxes so far in her life. She grabbed this one and sank to the floor in the middle of the room.

Jillian opened the box and out fell photos from the last few years of her life; photos of her and Jake at Evans Enterprises parties, photos of them with friends at other functions, photos of just them for press shots, single photos of each of them at the lake, at the park, being silly, magazine and newspaper articles about them together, about Jake's success, about the opening of her business.

    She softly uttered "No more….no more….no more…." She rocked back and forth as she sat on the floor clutching the photo and sobbed. No more…

CHAPTER EIGHTEEN

Richard looked down at Jillian sitting on the floor. He sighed. He really had no idea how he was going to handle this one. Sure he was a pro at war, at diffusing caustic situations, at killing the enemy; but when it came to consoling his Jilly, things were different. Okay Dad, help me out here; God, angels, anyone.

He looked more intently at her. She still had no clue he was even there. She was lost in whatever she was sobbing about. Then he saw the photographs and knew it had something to do with Jake. She just sat there, rocking gently back and forth, head hung down, clutching something to her chest, tears streaming down her cheeks and onto the photos and papers in front of her.

"Jilly?" he said quietly and slowly began approaching her so as not to startle her. She raised her tear stained face and his heart broke just looking at her. He saw the anguish, the lack of sleep, the red puffy eyes and mournful expression. He continued to slowly walk over to her and crouched down to her level and finally just sat down opposite her, not wanting to sit on the photos, not wanting to get too close, too soon.

"Honey, what is going on? What are you so upset about? What are you holding onto?" Richard placed a hand on her knee. She sobbed more and still continued rocking. This girl, his best female friend, was in the midst of a break down and he was clueless as to what brought it on or what to do next.

"Jillian", Richard's voice was firmer, stronger, yet with a soft compassion. "Talk to me!" he said, almost demanding at that point. She looked at him and shook her head and cried harder, still clutching the photograph tightly to her breast.

Richard got up and went into the kitchen and put a kettle of water on. He prepared two cups. He knew Jillian well enough to know what she stocked in her kitchen for food and for drinks and he thought maybe hot chocolate might be in order at this point. He prepared the mugs, thought for a second and put in a little shot of peppermint schnapps in both mugs before grabbing a couple paper towels and then he went back into the living room, assuming his position across from her on the floor. He put a paper towel on her knee and tried handing her the mug of steaming liquid topped with melting marshmallows.

"Jilly, I am not leaving you until I know you are alright." He reached over and wiped her tear stained face with his paper towel.

She grabbed the mug he handed her. Jillian dropped the photo she had been holding and put both hands around the mug. It felt good to her hands. She felt so utterly empty, so desolate, and so cold. Is this what death felt like? If it was she certainly didn't want to have any part of it. Richard noticed as the photo fell, it was the photo of the very first business dinner she and Jake attended. Jake was in a black tux and Jilly in a beautiful red sequined dress with a smile as bright as a Vegas marquee.

They sat in silence for the next thirty minutes. Jillian's sobs dissipated as she nursed her hot chocolate sip by sip. The quiet was deafening, almost eerie. The only sound heard was the chime of the Anniversary clock on the fireplace mantle every fifteen minutes. Richard looked at the clock. 4:30 a.m. He sighed.

"Honey, I hate to be an ass about this, but you need to get this out. Whatever is bothering you, you need to hear the words so it can set you free. I care about you, Jilly, and I hate seeing you in this state. Please, tell me what is wrong, so I can help you, so I can fix it. Please." Richard pleaded with her.

Jillian put her hand on Richard's knee, leaned forward and looked at him with her red, swollen, grief stricken eyes. "Richard, he's gone."

"Who's gone? Honey, what are you talking about?" Richard put his other hand on top of hers and began stroking it with his thumb.

"Jake. Jake is gone." She started tearing up again and her breaths became gulping gasps of air.

"No, Jilly, no more tears right now." He reached his hands up and held her face, searching her eyes for some clue to what she was talking about. "Tell me what is going on." He put emphasis on each word as he spoke it.

"Oh, God, Richard, it...it's just horrible. I don't know where to start." She sniffed, and reached for the tissues on the couch behind her, but Richard beat her to it, handing her the box. Jillian blew her nose and wiped her tears, holding onto the used tissues. "The night you dropped me off after our boat outing. Joni called. Said Jake had not made his flight. She was crying."

Her short sentences were annoying, but Richard knew that she was fighting crying again so he didn't press it. "She said that Jake had died. I put my shoes on. I…I…I drove over there. I didn't believe it. I knew he was in some sleazy hotel with some other woman. I knew if he were dead I would feel it in here."

She pointed to her heart and continued. "I got there and Andy had his arm around Joni and she had been crying. That's…that's when I knew something was terribly wrong. Joni…she told me that Jake gave a great presentation and they dismissed him and he was at the airport and taken to a Tokyo hospital and the doctors couldn't revive him and…and he died. Richard, what am I going to do? He died alone, Richard. He died alone." Her fast talking hadn't kept the tears at bay, she began weeping again.

Richard carefully moved the photographs out of the way and moved over beside her. He pulled her into his arms and just held her. Jillian's body was shaking from the violent sobs. Her soul hurt to the very core of her being. Richard kissed the top of her head and smoothed her hair out with his hand. He talked to her as calmly as he could to reassure her that it was not her fault.

"You are going to handle this with the grace you always do. And I am going to be right by your side." Richard promised. "I know you feel it is partially your fault and you are going through the mountain of 'what ifs' in your mind, but honey, none of this is your fault. It can't help but hurt after the years you were with him. But, Jilly, you know what he was doing the last few months. And if the truth be told, he was doing this all along. I won't speak badly about the dead, I know he had his good points, but I am glad it is over, for your sake, and I'm sorry you're hurting.

"I'm truly sorry he was alone, but Honey there was nothing you could have done to stop what happened. What happened could have happened anywhere at any time." Richard tried to be as reassuring as he could be. This was all so out of his comfort zone.

"What's next? How can I help?"

The weariness in her voice was staggering. "I told Joni I would get a hold of Stan Austin, Jake's former partner, and see what needs to be done regarding Evans Enterprises. His body is being shipped back and should arrive at week's end, hopefully, but it could also take longer. I suppose there should be a funeral or memorial service or something. Jake has no family. I…me…I was the closest thing to family he had." She started crying again. "Richard, what am I going to do? What is appropriate? Should I just let Joni handle it all?"

Richard had never cared much for Jake, but he would swallow any pride or jealousy to help out his friend. "Jilly, we will do this together and I will help as much as I can. Let me call Stan and figure out when and where the funeral should be. You help Joni deal with what she needs to deal with. I'm glad you have good people working for you that can handle the flower shop right now. I'm going to give Alex a call and let him know what's going on so he can take care of the shop for a few days until all this is over." Jillian started to protest, but he put his finger to her lips. "No protesting. I'll also put a call in to Ginger about food for the funeral. Honey, it is all going to be okay. Please just let me help. I'm here for you."

Jillian heard those words as they bounced around in the back of her mind. They were the same words she had heard from Richard when Brett died. They were the same words she heard from him when she planned her parents' funerals. Again the words "let me help, I'm here for you" reverberated through her entire being. Her shoulders sagged and she gave in to the thoughts. Richard truly was the only one who had always been there for her; the good, the bad and the really ugly moments of her life. And this one was the ugliest.

Richard kissed the top of her head again and sat with his arms wrapped around her until the night conceded to dawn's sunlight, which poured through the windows and bathed their shoulders in its warmth.

I will do whatever it takes to get her though this. Richard knew in his heart of hearts that the feelings he had had for Jillian all these years were finally coming to the surface and now certainly was NOT the time to deal with them. He wondered if and when he would ever deal with them. The last thing Jilly needed was to be invited into his hell of murderous plagued dreams and more sadness.

The warmth from the sun felt good on his back, muscles of said back in spasms from sitting in the same position for so long. He wasn't going to disturb this woman in his arms. The sobs had finally stopped and judging from her even shallow breathing she had fallen asleep.

Richard looked at his watch. It was 7:15 now and not too early to make some phone calls, not to mention he really HAD to get up from this position he'd sat in for the past few hours. He reached behind him for the pillow that had supported him against the couch and gently slid his arms from around Jillian, moving slowly so as to hopefully not awaken her. He slid down low enough on the floor that she slid with him and at that point he replaced his body with the pillow. She curled up into a little ball and Richard just looked at her. She so needed sleep. He was going to try his damnedest to be quiet so he wouldn't wake her.

It was difficult for Richard to get up from the floor. He hadn't sat so long in one position, let alone on the floor, in a long time. He got on his hands and knees and used the couch to slowly push himself up to a standing position. There was a tattered quilt on the back of the couch and Richard grabbed it and gently set the cover over Jillian. Richard, old boy, you are too old for this shit, he thought as he walked toward the kitchen with the dirty hot chocolate mugs.

The bathroom was just down the hall and he knew Jillian wouldn't mind if he showered to wake up. He would make it quick and then make the phone calls from the back bedroom so as not to disturb her.

Richard spent a lot longer in the shower than he had intended. The hot water ran over his head and down his sore, tired body. He just couldn't understand a man like Jake. In many ways the guy had everything any man could dream of; a successful business, a car for every day of the week, money to burn, and a gorgeous woman on his arm who loved him and catered to his every whim. If only HE could be that lucky.

A towel hung on a rack by the shower door and Richard grabbed it and hastily ran it across his wet body. He put his clothes back on and made his way to the bedroom and closed the door, leaving it ajar, just in case Jillian woke up.

"Alex?" Richard inquired of the male voice on the other end of the phone.

"Hey, Uncle Richard, what's up?" Alex was always so wide awake and so positive in the mornings; another thing he wished was one of his fortes.

"Listen, your mom has had quite a ni..." Alex stopped Richard in mid- sentence.

"What's wrong with Mom? Is she okay? Uncle Richard, what's going on?" Alex's questions came fast and furious.

"Calm down, son, and listen. I've been with your mom at the apartment above the flower shop since about 3 a.m. I fell asleep at the store and when I locked up I looked across the street and noticed the light on upstairs. I went over to make sure things were okay, you know?"

"So, is Mom okay?" Alex persisted.

"Yes, Alex, she is sleeping right now. I told her I would call you and let you know she won't be in to work today. You need to open the shop and let the other workers know it may be a couple days. She has had quite a shock, Alex.

"We got back from boating night before last and it was late when I dropped your mom off. She evidently got a phone call from Jake's secretary and she drove over to her place." Richard paused.

"Alex, Jake died in Tokyo."

"Oh, hell!"

"It is really important right now that we do all we can to help your mom get through this. She is not in a good place. Even though she and Jake weren't together, you don't just toss those years of love in the trash, ya know?"

"What do you want me to do?"

"Alex, if you could just make sure the shop is running that would be huge. Your mom needs some rest. This was quite a shock and she finally came to terms with her feelings for Jake tonight. I found her on the floor in the living room of the apartment sobbing clutching a photo of her and Jake at some function. She sobbed for hours and finally was so tired she fell asleep. I tried my hardest to be quiet and got her comfortable by the fireplace and went to the back bedroom to make some calls."

"Uncle Richard, I really don't know what Mom, what we, would do without you. Thank you for always being there for us." The concern in Alex's voice tugged at Richard's heart, making his feelings for Jillian even more real.

"Just do what you can, son. I know her biggest fear is that the shop runs like normal and you are the only one who knows how to do that. Just make it happen, okay? I need to call Ginger and get some funeral things settled. I'll be in touch." And with that Richard was on to the next task at hand; calling Stan and Ginger to set in motion the plans for Jake's funeral. That wasn't a job he was looking forward to at all. But he'd be damned if he was going to see Jillian go through all of that again by herself.

Richard looked at his watch. Damn, it was time to go to his store. He took his cell phone and called Alex again.

"Alex, one more thing. Would you please stop by the antique store and let whoever is there know I won't be in today that something came up. I will check in with them later. Thanks, son."

Alex agreed to what was asked and Richard was off the hook. He was not going to leave Jillian. He lay back on the bed and within minutes he was asleep.

CHAPTER NINETEEN

Jake had outlined precise directions on how his death/funeral should be handled. He wanted a party in the style of an old fashioned Irish wake: a party, no sadness, no funeral rather a memorial service in the arboretum at Evans Enterprises. After the autopsy confirmed the death was due to "natural causes, a month to the day of his death the memorial service happened. Many business associates from abroad came to pay their respects, as did many of the locals. Joni greeted the mourners at the door and ushered them to the memorial table where the "corporate" 11x 14 portrait of Jake was displayed.

Jillian had made a garland from red roses, myrtle and variegated boxwood that surrounded the urn that held Jake's ashes and set at the base of the portrait. It was a nice tribute. There was a simple but elegant program that the secretaries had put together that was being handed to those who came before they sat down. It outlined Jake's business accomplishments throughout his life and thanked those who helped with the service today. Stan Austin was to be the first in a long line of speakers to voice his memories of Jake. There was no music, no religious presence, just friends and associates in a social setting that could seem like a normal networking party under normal circumstances.

Stan walked up to the microphone in front of the rows of chairs. He cleared his throat several times before reaching the podium. There was so much to say, but Stan was a man of little words so his portion of the eulogy was short and directly to the point.

As she heard Stan begin his speech with a thank you for those attending, Jillian wondered what would be said if Jake's dad still was alive. What would he have said? How would he have handled Jake's behavior? John was so much more personable than Stan and certainly the one who made Austin and Evans so successful. Jake grew up just like his dad in all ways but one. She sighed and turned her full attention to what Stan was saying. She would never understand where the womanizing came from.

"Jake had a vision for Evans Enterprises that I could not see," Stan began as he placed his hands on each side of the podium. "I am very thankful that he bought out my interest and ran with it and made it what it is today. His interest in international holdings has made this company a viable voice in Japan and Europe. Evans Enterprises will be an entity to deal with for a long time to come. Jake, you son-of-a-bitch, you achieved your dream. And, in the end, that is the best that any of us can ever hope to do."

Stan Austin concluded with a nod and stepped away from the microphone and joined his grieving, pregnant daughter, placing an arm around her shoulders making her cry all the more. Stan knew how much Sindra cared for Jake, loved working for Jake. They were like brother and sister, he thought. Stan silently wished Jake was still alive. He knew that Jake could reach Sindra as no one else could.

Sindra had gotten "knocked-up" at college and refused to discuss it with anyone, saying it just hurt too much and she wouldn't reveal who the father was because it would just upset everyone all the more. Although she was only 6 months pregnant, she looked full term. Stan was beside himself as to what to say or do to console her at this point so he just walked away to converse with another colleague, leaving the poor girl just standing there, her arms clutching the baby blue shawl that was wrapped around her shoulders.

Several other business associates, including Mr. Tomeiki, joined in the Celebration of Life for Jake stating remembrances of his goodness, how he was all about team work and how he ran a visionary corporation with loyal employees who strived to achieve what their CEO set out for them.

Joni spoke of how wonderful the employer/employee relationship was that she had with Jake and how she respected him as a person and as her boss. She brought up that he always called her "tiger" because of her way of dealing with the clients.

It was a moving service celebrating Jake's accomplishments and the Board of Directors promised to "hold fast to the dream for the future of Evans Enterprises". The Board of Directors in a special meeting after the news of Jake's death unanimously voted to ask Stan Austin to come back as temporary CEO until Jake's will was read and his wishes could be carried out.

Everyone knew it would take some time to sort through things and notify those who were specified in the will. There were specific instructions about where the will was to be read and who was to be in attendance. Jake requested The Board, of course, to be present as well as Stan, Sindra, Joni and Jillian. They were all to be there. When Jillian heard this she was puzzled at that particular assortment of people, but would attend because it was Jake's last wishes. It was strange to Jillian that even in death Jake included her in his business. There was an eeriness that shrouded her making her think Jake knew he was dying.

Jillian stood on the patio by the food tables, her arms wrapped around her waist in a hugging fashion. She drew the black wool blazer closer around her. She looked around the arboretum. The late afternoon autumn sun brought out the vibrant colors of the beautiful hardy mum bushes that were in full bloom as well as the pampas grass. The grounds were in full bloom and a beautiful burst of fall colors.

Mr. Tomeiki and Stan were deeply engaged in conversation she noticed, then turned and saw Joni and some of the employees reminiscing about some recent events. There were other small groups of people here and there. For the most part the service was done. She didn't cherish the thought of hanging around for the next couple of hours but she would do it because it was for Jake.

Jillian looked at the buffet tables. Thanks to Ginger and Jordan she didn't have to worry about the food, or cleaning up afterward...thank God for that! David and Denise had brought food from Turner's as well and would help with the clean-up. Jillian smiled. Bless Richard! He had talked with Stan and planned the service. He arranged the catering. He talked Alex into manning the shop. It amazed her that Richard was always there for her any time, all the time. So were Ginger, Jordan, David and Denise. Her friends meant the world to her.

There were no tears today. Jillian slowly walked over to the memorial table. With the index finger of her right hand she traced the frame of Jake's portrait and sighed. "Oh Jake" she thought "I pray you are happy where ever you are and at peace." She touched her fingers to her lips then to Jake's. She straightened the garland, her hand lingering on the urn that contained his ashes.

A large hand covered hers and she instantly felt a warm body behind her. "Are you okay?" It was Richard. Jillian smiled, leaned her head back into his chest, and without turning around replied "Yes. I truly am going to be okay

****

Three months had passed since Jake's memorial service. His ashes buried at a local mausoleum; other matters of business taken care of and now the finale. Jillian checked her watch. It was 6:55 p.m. and the will reading was to begin promptly at 7. She parked in the lot at the end of the building instead of in front; partly because she didn't want to see Jake's parking spot, but mostly because she felt the short walk might clear her head and heart a bit before she became a part of whatever it was she was there for.

It was a cold, drizzly evening; very typical of winter in the Pacific Northwest. As she entered the building and made her way down the hall an eerie feeling came over her. For a moment, it felt as if Jake was holding her hand, walking beside her, like he had so many times before.

Jillian opened the door to the main conference room at Evans Enterprises. The lighting was dim and she nodded to John Simpson, the current Board Chairman, and made her way around the massive table to the last open chair. John, because of his position with Evans Enterprises, sat at the head of the table. He was a retired attorney and had been legal counsel for Evans Enterprises for as long as she had known Jake; and John was also the Executor of Jake's estate. It was only natural that he be the one to read the will. John put his glasses on and began.

"As we begin this adventure, I thank you for being here. It was Jake's wishes that you all be here collectively for the reading instead of being contacted individually." John was a bit antsy as evidenced by the continual shaking of his feet under the table. "Let's begin, shall we?" John grabbed the stack of papers that were in front of him, positioning them so he could more easily see the words.

"This is the reading of the Last Will and Testament of Jake Evans." John peered over the top of his glasses as he read on. "I, Jake Evans, being of sound mind declare this to be my last will and testament. I direct that my just debts, funeral expenses and all medical expenses be paid from proceeds from my estate."

John continued reading "Any and all digital assets found on any electronic devices including computers, shall remain property of Evans Enterprises and be accessible to the CEO, board chairperson and secretary of the CEO. John Simpson shall act as Executor of my estates, both corporate and personal. He shall have the right to administer my estates without unnecessary intervention by the probate court. And when all duties have been performed and carried out as set forth herein, John Simpson is relieved of his duties.

"Stan Austin, should he still be living and agreeable to this request, is hereby appointed as acting CEO until the Board of Directors of Evans Enterprises shall elect by secret ballot the new CEO."

John coughed, cleared his throat and drank from a glass of water before he continued reading the articles of how things should and would be carried out by him regarding the will and making sure that all that was contained in the will would be done to Jake's specifications.

John paused from the will to give a warning to the room. "In this next section, I will not break once I start reading the disbursements of property. I would ask that you all be quiet because I am sure there are going to be surprises that may shock most of you. I will be available for questions at the conclusion of the will reading, so let's hold off any inquiries until then." He peered over his glasses and scanned the room, looking directly at each person there. "Your cooperation is much appreciated."

John cleared his throat, once again, like a man not looking forward to the hard task ahead, heaved a heavy sigh and started reading. "I hereby direct my estate to be disbursed as follows: to the current Board of Directors of Evans Enterprises, I leave 33% of Evans Enterprises to be split equally, including any and all monetary assets and interest from profits. You earned every percent by giving me 100% of your loyalty and time. The chairman of the Board of Directors will be elected by the Board of Directors and the owners of Evans Enterprises and shall act as the new CEO. The CEO will be responsible to the Board for any and all decisions made on behalf of Evans Enterprises.

"To Jillian Halloran, the eternal love of my life," John rushed through the words just slightly, giving away a bit of his own discomfort. "I leave the proceeds from three life insurance policies. Jillian, this should be enough for you to maintain the property of your shop and home as well as be enough so you don't stand in want of anything.

"To my faithful secretary, my right hand girl Friday, Joni Phillips, I leave 33% interest in Evans Enterprises including any and all monetary assets and interest from profits. As long as you work for the company you will be a permanent member of the Board of Directors, and serve as the secretary to the Board. Honey, you deserve this and so much more for putting up with my tirades over all the years.

"This is for you and Andy to live a secure life. Make me proud, Tiger, and carry on the high standards that make Evans Enterprises what it is today. I also decree that you are to stay on as the secretary to the new CEO. You know how this company works and how I want it run. You will be given 20% cost of living increases to your salary every January until you decide it is time for you to leave Evans Enterprises.

"To my little Sindra, I leave my condo and my vintage automobile collection. You can sell the ones you don't want but the proceeds from the auto sales will go into an escrow account for the care of my child." John paused when there were several surprised gasps, though surprisingly the room did well in keeping muttering to a minimum.

"To my unborn child I leave 34% of and controlling interest in Evans Enterprises. The money accrued from this percentage is to be held in escrow until the child is 21 years of age. At which time, if said child expresses interest in Evans Enterprises, he or she will be named permanent CEO and retain the right to make decisions on behalf of this corporation. The interest from the escrow account may be used for necessary accrued expenses for the care and welfare of my child. Even though I am not present physically, you know I will be there with you, watching over you, protecting you.

"In the event that my child wishes to not be involved in Evans Enterprises, the controlling interest will be sold to the Board of Directors who will then have controlling interest in the corporation. My child will still retain 32% of any and all monetary proceeds.

"I humbly decree these to be my last wishes. If you are reading this it means I am in a better place, hopefully. It's been a wild ride and you know I will walk the halls of Evans every now and again just because I can. I hereto set my signature to this document and declare it legal and binding."

CHAPTER TWENTY

The reading of Jake's will came as quite a shock to everyone in the board room. No one was more surprised than Jillian when the words "and to my unborn child..." were read. It sure made Stan sit up and take notice! Now he knew why his daughter had been so guarded with the information of who was the father of her child.

Sindra was due any day with the birth of the child she was carrying. She looked so sad. Jillian wondered exactly how she would handle the stipulations set forth in Jake's will. Thankfully her father was well versed in legalities and could help her sort things out.

It was a miracle that Sindra had told Jake right away, within weeks of finding out about the pregnancy so his will reflected that fact. There were way too many secrets. Jillian shook her head and pondered over all of the "secrets" from the past few years.

There had to have been women everywhere, in the States and abroad. Dorian came to mind. She wondered why nothing was left to her. Jillian wondered if anyone had contacted Dorian to let her know what had happened. Maybe that was part of Joni's job, going through the Rolodex and online lists and notifying people of Jake's death. It certainly wasn't her place to do that. Not now anyway.

Women all over the country partook of Jake's advances and charm; as evidenced by the pregnancy of his ex-partner's daughter. Jillian raised an eyebrow. Amazing things happen over a summer internship, she guessed. It was totally Jake, though, totally how he operated. It was his love-them-and-leave- them mentality. She was just thankful that this time he was responsible enough to do something good for a change!

As soon as John concluded the will reading, the Board members and Joni and Stan all began hashing out a plan for the future of Evans Enterprises. Jillian noticed how bittersweet this all had been today. From death to new life of a company that would face the future with the innovation new blood would bring, not to mention the birth of Jake's heir.

Sindra shyly smiled at Jillian as they both left at the same time. Jillian hugged the girl and wished her well. What else could she do? Jake had seen to her financial well-being and that of his child. She would have a place to live and a car for every day of the week if she wanted. Jillian knew she was being catty about it, but come on, really? Just how many vehicles does one person need? Especially a pregnant twenty year old!

At this point, Jillian struggled with whether she should even be nice enough to Sindra to say "if you need anything, call" or just leave it alone. There was no way at twenty she would have been ready to have a child, let alone a child with this much prospective money and power. And, having someone there to help or to talk with through the whole process would be necessary for emotional sanity.

Every time Jillian thought about someone else carrying Jake's child…or children, judging from Sindra's size, her heart hurt. She and Jake had talked on many occasions about adopting, about marriage, about growing old together. The candle flame of that dream was snuffed out and now only a memory. It was dark in the recesses of that box where Jillian had filed those memories and she just simply could not go there right now. It was difficult enough to process the words she heard tonight without borrowing trouble from the past.

Then there was the fact from earlier; Jake had left HER the life insurance policies, all of them! She had no clue what that meant, but Stan and John both assured her that she needed to find a reputable investment guru because by the end of the week checks would be issued and mailed to her, totaling millions, along with the appropriate paperwork from Jake's estate.

Jillian just shook her head at the thought. With all that went on today, this was the last thing she wanted to think about. She made her way through the empty halls of Evans Enterprises, pausing here and there for not more than a couple minutes to etch in her mind different memories. Once at the double glass doors, she made her way out to the patio of the arboretum.

The light drizzle continued and she tightened the scarf around her neck and pulled the coat collar up around her as a shield from the drizzle. She walked across to the bench by the fountain and sat down, her head still swimming.

She didn't care that it was still drizzling or that it was cold. She just wanted a quiet moment to breathe in the events that would so drastically change her life. Jillian's thoughts wandered to the good times with Jake; to the times of concerts and movies and snuggling on the couch with a bowl of popcorn they shared. Those treasured times of sweet kisses and tender love making until the wee hours of the morning and the formal dinners and parties on behalf of the company he so loved. If only he could have remained faithful to her. If only he didn't have the need for more than her. If only things could have been different. Jake may still be alive and they may have salvaged the relationship and turned it around so that it was as it was in the beginning. Who am I kidding?

Sitting here in the garden of Evans Enterprises allowed Jillian's thoughts to wander to the day of the memorial service. She remembered there were people milling around, mainly those who were designated to clean up. She thought about the precise eulogy Stan gave, the kind words of Mr. Tomeiki, the heart wrenching tearful goodbye from Joni. She was so self-absorbed in her thoughts that she didn't notice Richard had sat down by her on the bench.

Startled by the presence of someone else invading her space, she jumped and turned to see her best friend by her side. "Hi, kiddo. How ya doin?" he asked with a concerned tone in his voice that warmed her heart.

Jillian wistfully smiled and grabbed Richard's hand. "What are you doing here? I'm okay, really. I wish you would stop worrying about me."

Richard's deep chuckle made her smile. He began, "I knew that tonight was the night of the will reading and I thought maybe you might need a friend. John told me you were out here." Richard tightened the grip on her hand.

"And, seems to me, remember when I was in the hospital after I got home from Nam? I believe we had this very same conversation however I was the one who told YOU not to worry about me. Guess what, kiddo? It ain't happening!"

Jillian smiled and chuckled at his statement. She remembered she had been so concerned, so worried about him when he returned. His injuries were not physical but the emotional trauma had cut deep and it was very real just the same.

"So, are you going to tell me what went on in there? You seem in a different land right now, Jilly. What's up?" Richard folded his fingers in hers and held her hand.

"Well, let me tell you," she began. "It has been a very interesting evening so far, to say the least." Jillian turned so she was more directly facing Richard before she continued. "The board members received 33% of Evans Enterprises and the task of voting in a new CEO from the board! Joni received 33% of the company as well..."

Richard interrupted "Oh, don't tell me he left YOU controlling interest..."

Jillian cut him off before he could finish, putting her hand up to make him be quiet. "Just wait, it gets better. He left 34% and controlling interest for his unborn child to be held in escrow until the child reaches 21 years of age. And he left Sindra his condo and all of his vehicles."

A quizzical expression and an "are-you-kidding" type smile crossed

Richard's face. You could tell the wheels were just working overtime in his head as he tried to figure it all out.

"Okay, wait a minute, his unborn child? And who is the lucky "mommy" of this unborn child? And why would he leave his cars to a teenager? What the hell is she going to do with his classic car collection? She is barely old enough to drive, right?" Richard inquired.

"Yup. Well, seems he got Sindra Austin pregnant sometime this spring. She evidently told him right away, within weeks of finding out she was pregnant and once he knew, he made changes to his will to include the child, his child. Sindra is close to 20 now, I think, but that doesn't matter. At least Jake did the right thing and provided for his child, and its mother." Jillian explained.

Taking in a big breath and blowing it out, she tightened her grip on Richard's hand then continued. "And, he left me all of his life insurance policies. According to Stan and John they total millions."

"No shit?" Richard sat farther back on the bench and ran his free hand through his would-be hair, his face showing obvious surprise. "He got Sindra pregnant?" he chuckled. "Oh, Stan must love that! Well, it sounds like Jake at least provided for her and the baby. That was the first good thing he has done in a very long time!"

"Richard, what the hell am I going to do with his life insurance proceeds, Richard? I mean, you know how I live. You know that I'm a simple gal who just wants to play with flowers and be left alone. I put most of Brett's life insurance into CD's and have been living off the interest from that for years. I guess maybe now I can transfer the money in those CD's to the boys; you know, split it equally between them. I'm not sure; I just don't know what I should be doing with Jake's money." Jillian shook her head and shrugged her shoulders.

Richard squeezed her hand and released it. "Well, it is no longer 'Jake's money'" he said making quote marks with his fingers. "It's yours now. The first thing you need to do is find someone who can invest the majority of it for you. I would say if you wanted to be generous with what you get, you could set up accounts for the boys so they would be taken care of until they figure life out, but since you just mentioned dividing Brett's money, maybe this can just be for you, you know? Then you can use the interest from these investments to fix up that apartment above your store or buy a new building or a house or whatever you want. He wanted you to have this so you wouldn't have to struggle. I admire him for that. Even in his death he is showing his love and devotion for you."

"But, why, why even after I kicked him out for being such a lecher would he still name me as one of his beneficiaries? It just creeps me out that he'd do that. You know, we never talked about money. Money never seemed to matter to Jake. He always had enough to get what he wanted…and who he wanted. I never dreamed he was worth so much, you know? I never looked at him in that light; that he was this corporate big-wig with all the bucks in the world. I just saw him as Jake, plain, common, Jake. Yet, in his death I find out he was anything but common."

Jillian slid over closer to Richard and put her head on his shoulder. She linked her fingers in his again. It felt so right to be sitting here like this sharing her soul with this man as she often did. "Thank you, Richard, thank you for always being the voice of reason in my life. I don't know what I'd do without you."

"You know what, Jilly? That's something you'll never have to worry about. I'm not going anywhere." Richard assured her and brought their linked fingers to his mouth and kissed her hand. He sighed and leaned his head to hers so they touched. No, he wasn't going anywhere. And, at this moment, he vowed in his heart he would do anything and everything he could to keep this woman in his life for the rest of his life.

EXCERPT FROM
MYSTIC CAPERS
Book 2 of the Acorn Hills Series

"And it is my great pleasure to introduce world renowned Executive Chef, Henri Choinard, Director of the famous French School of Culinary and Pastry Arts, who will do the honors of presenting this year's winner of the prestigious Donovan Award for overall excellence." Peter Hammond began.

"This year has been so exciting! There have been so many five star experts who have won this award over the years, and the winner this year is another who far surpasses the meaning of 'pastry chef'." Peter turned his attention to the audience, acknowledging the entrants who had given their best shot at what was tossed their way this week. He nodded and continued, "I wish all of the contestants the very best luck.

"Now, I will turn this over to Henri for the award presentations." Peter announced. Peter, who never had a hair out of place, who looked like a million bucks in his customary black tux had been the emcee for these local pastry/baking/food competitions for years and took as much pride in the winners as the winners themselves.

He owned two Five Star restaurants and a ribs place in Acorn Hills. Peter was a well-known, well-respected chef himself and loved the spotlight whenever he could be in it. He was the type of a person who could smile and you instantly saw the little glitter shine from one of his teeth!

He handed the microphone to Chef Choinard who bowed to him and gave the customary kiss-on-each-cheek greeting and took his place center stage to begin the award ceremony.

Chef H., as Ginger remembered calling him, was a rotund little

Frenchman. He reminded her of the man in the Chef Boyardee commercials. He had a very gentle demeanor and expression. But he had a temper too, when things were not going as he wished.

"Merci, Peter. Let's give him a big thank you for his years of work with the Donovan Award competition." Chef Henri slightly raised his arms and began clapping and the crowd erupted with applause and whistles and shouts of thanks that lasted more than it should have.

Ginger smiled and stood, joining the others in their gratitude of this man, but really wished they would just get on with it! She was tired. It had been a long 3 days of competition. She just wanted to go home, kick off her shoes, make some hot chocolate and snuggle her man. However, these award ceremonies seemed to take longer and longer every time she entered and it made her wonder why she felt the need to be a part of them. Yet if she was going to make a name for herself here in Acorn Hills, she was going to have to do all she could, and that meant entering competitions like this one.

Chef Choinard waved his hands for people to quiet down and take their seats, yet it still took several minutes to get that accomplished. She giggled to herself, maybe the others were as tired of sitting as she was and were just taking advantage of the opportunity to stand and stretch before all the awards were given.

The competitors were seated at tables that were front and center of microphone Chef Henri was using. It made it very convenient to get up and get to the stage to accept your award, if you were one of the lucky ones.

"You know," Chef Henri began, his heavy French accent making it difficult to understand his words at times. "Eet takes so much to enter competish-i-ons like this one. There are three categorees; Best pastry, Best plating, and Best flavor. These have already been judged. The competish-i-on this year has been incredible and I hold in my hand the results of the judging. Bonne Chance a tous!" He nodded to the crowd.

He then turned the paper over he was holding and began reading, "In third place, placing 3rd in pastry, 2nd in plating and 3rd in flavor, Senor Jose Arina!" Jose made his way to the stage and proudly bowed as the medal was placed around his neck and the crowd erupted again with shouts of appreciation.

Peter began "Jose owns a very upscale Mexican/Mariachi restaurant in Coral Knoll, but also serves the best pastries of any restaurant of that genre in the area. Once again, congratulations, Mr. Jose Arina!" Applause erupted.

Chef Henri looked like a proud "papa" as he introduced the winners. He continued, "In 2nd place and overall champion in the chocolate competition, Monseiur Dickie Mason!"

Mason made his way to the stage while Peter added to what was already said. "Dickie also placed 2rd in pastry, 3rd in plating and 2nd in flavor. Let's hear it for Dickie Mason!" Mason made his way to the stage and greeted Jose and also bowed to receive his medal and customary cheek kissing from Chef Henri.

Dickie, too, was no stranger to the food wars of competition. He was in his early 60's and quite the chocolatier and blown candy maker. He was the instructor for the continuing education class Ginger took on candy making. She learned a lot about the technique of blown sugar. She was truly happy for him getting 2nd place.

Ginger stood and applauded Dickie as he accepted his medal. He was her most stiff competition. It must be the champagne because she giggled at the thought of the words running through her head. She was sure that Dickie couldn't make anything stiff except egg whites even if he tried! He was a very talented chocolatier and one of the nicest guys you'd ever meet. Just a little, um, eccentric. Yes, that was it, eccentric.

She smiled and looked around the room. So many other talented chefs were at this event. She spotted Jacque Monet, the head chef of the Acorn Hills Regency, a five star hotel. Over in the corner behind him was Bruce Dinsmore, the head chef of Baklava, who was last year's winner. These men were so far above her, so out of her league.

She was a fish out of her pond trying to swim with the big guys. She simply felt she didn't stand a chance of winning this year. She sat back down and Jordan grabbed her hand. He sensed her disappointment, could feel the wind just taken out of her sails for this whole thing.

In her heart she was fully prepared to lose, yet again, but with each competition, she gained valuable experience, and that is what counted. Just once, though, she wished she could have the limelight of prestige that came with winning one of these "medal" competitions. She audibly sighed, making Jordan bring her hand up to his lips and kiss it as he put his other arm around the back of her chair in a reassuring gesture. Ginger smiled feebly at Jordan and turned her attention back to center stage.

After the crowd settled down and it was quiet as could be, Chef Henri began the announcement of the "big" award.

"It is an honour to announce zee First Place weener of zees' year's Donovan award." Chef Henri began.

"Zees Chef has proven time and again how pastry should look and taste. I am so proud to say that zees chef is one of my star students from zee past and has achieved first place judging in all three categories of zees competish-i-on." Ginger looked quizzically at Jordan after that statement. As far as she knew she was the only one from this area that had attended his school. Her heart was in her throat.

Chef Henri continued, "Her lemon curd tart took best of show in pastry and flavor and her whimsical 'chocolate with a swirl' captured best plating. It is with great pleasure I introduce you to this year's gagnant du grand prix, Mademoiselle Ginger Farnsworth."

The room went crazy with shouts of joy and whistles when Ginger's name was announced.

She froze in her seat. Her hand instinctively went to cover her mouth. "Oh my God!" She thought, "Really?" HER lemon curd tart? HER chocolate swirl? Oh holy hell! She had just won! She had just won the Donovan Award and, more importantly, along with it a check for $20,000! She was stunned!

She heard the cheering and clapping and she saw Jordan next to her trying to get her out of her seat to walk up to the stage to accept her award. She felt like she was watching Robin Williams as he re-enacted winning his Oscar. Time stopped for her and it felt like she was moving in very slow motion as she made her way to the stage. Cameras were flashing, people were cheering and applauding; and to have to speak following this; sure that was going to be a happening thing!

She moved toward the stage. The lights made her shimmer from head to toe in the form fitting copper sequined gown and set her auburn hair on fire. The very expensive designer heels that matched her dress made her feet feel like lead. This was the only "good" party dress she owned and the only time she wore it was at the dinners of the competitions she entered. She was grateful no one noticed she wore the same thing to all of them, and if they did, they didn't say anything about it to her. She was amazed that she didn't trip over anything on her way to the stage. She was NOT used to wearing shoes like this or clothes like this. She was strictly a jeans and sweatshirt kind of girl.

She got to the bottom of the steps to the stage and Peter Hammond offered his hand and helped her up the stairs to the microphone where Chef Henri was waiting.

"Ms. Farnsworth, congratulash-i-ons on being this year's Donovan Award winner." He placed the gold medal around her neck and gave her the oversized check and of course did the kissy cheek thing. She would never understand that as long as she lived. A hug and a handshake would suffice, but to the French that was as much a part of their culture as the handshake and hugs were of ours. The crowd erupted again and she saw her beloved Jordan taking pictures with a smile so broad that it put Peter's to shame! Chef Henri moved to the side and gestured for her to be center stage.

"Oh my God! I am honestly speechless! There are so many wonderful chefs in this room. Jose and Dickie congratulations to you both. It was such an honor to compete with you."

Ginger turned, nodded and placed her free hand over her heart. "To the judges and Chef Henri, merci." She bowed. "Thank you so much for your confidence in my abilities. I love to food. I love the smell of it, the texture of it, the way I can mold it the way I want it. You all know pastry is my first love, my favorite, and I love serving my customers what I feel are the very best pastries in all of Acorn Hills." Applause erupted again.

"This award means so much to me. I have entered so many competitions and this" she picked up the medal in her free hand and choked back tears. "It is the frosting on the cake, so to speak." The judges and other competitors chuckled at her pun.

"When I was in high school Home Economics I decided that I wanted to do something with my life passion; food. Little did I know that it would take me to Chef Henri's school in Dordogne, France. Ultimately what I learned there enabled me to open my own little catering shop and bakery."

"Jordan, love of my life," she blew him a kiss. "I thank you so much for believing in me and loving me through all of this because I certainly could not have done it without you." Ginger continued to hold her medal. "Again, thank you so much for this great honor." She nodded her head to the audience and cheers erupted as they stood in appreciation of her hard work.

And, right on cue, the music began signaling the ending of the ceremony. Tears were coming down her cheeks now, damn it. She tried so hard to not let that happen. Jose and Dickie and Peter and Chef Henri all hugged her. The judges made their way over to her, congratulating. The photographer for "Just Pastries", one of the major sponsors of the competition, was barking orders for the judges to get in line and Ginger to get in the center and Chef Henri to be on one side of her and Peter Hammond to be on the other side of her so the larger-than-life-sized check was stretched out between them with her in the middle.

And, Jordan, smiling and standing like a proud peacock winked and blew her a kiss. She smiled and the photographer snapped the picture. The story would be on page one of the Acorn Hills Chronicle tomorrow, not to mention her phone would not stop ringing and people would be lined up around the block to taste her pastries. Life cannot get much better than this she thought.

Jordan met her at the bottom of the stage steps. "Well, pumpkin, you did it." He picked her up and twirled in a circle with her in his arms. "I am so stinkin' proud of you!" He kissed her and continued to hold on to her. She wrapped her arms around Jordan's neck and just savored the moment. Her cheeks hurt so much from smiling. The adrenaline was still flowing from the excitement she felt from winning. The possibilities were swimming in her head of what to do with the money.

During the photo session, the "worker bees" had moved the tables and chairs into a more dance friendly set up. The DJ was busy setting things on what had been the head table up on the stage. Ginger was ready to "partay", as David would say. She wished David and Denise could be here to share this with them.

Jordan put her down and she immediately took off the heels. If she was going to dance the rest of the evening away, she was going to be comfortable. She grabbed Jordan's hand and headed back to one of the tables and put her shoes on a chair then dragged him out to the already crowded dance floor just as Kool and the Gang began singing "Celebrate Good Times, C'mon!" This truly was "good times". It was a night she would remember for a very long time.

Jordan had spoken to the DJ while she was finishing up the photos. They were both accomplished ballroom dancers (classes they decided to take to spend time together) and he wanted Ginger to really enjoy the night more with a special dance, just for them. After the current selection ended, the lights dimmed and the first notes of "Rainbow Connection" began. It was Ginger's all-time favorite song. Tears welled up in her eyes again as Jordan bowed to his lovely lady. How he loved this creature! She was glowing; the lighting made her skin flawless, her auburn curls framing her face and cascading over her shoulders, the strapless copper sequin-covered mermaid gown hugging her full figure. Jordan took Ginger's hand and led her in a foxtrot around the dance floor. Everyone stepped aside as they watched the couple glide around the room.

She was smiling so much her cheeks hurt. Jordan knew her so well…he always knew what she needed even before she knew! Their dance ended with a beautiful twirl and dip with Jordan bending over and kissing her before standing her back up. The crowd erupted with shouts of appreciation for the true art they just witnessed.

"Oh, Jordan," Ginger began. "This is incredible. All of it!" She placed her hand on his cheek and looked lovingly into his eyes. "Thank you. Thank you for being the man in my life. Thank you for sharing all the bad stuff and the good stuff." She threw her arms around his neck and just stood there swaying, hugging him. "I do love you so much," she whispered in his ear.

Another familiar tune began but she was oblivious to what was going on. She was just in her own little moment. She was amazed at the accomplishments she had achieved. She had "come into her own" as the old adage says, and she was going to relish every moment of it.